M000236380

LEADER'S GUIDE

Ellen A. Brubaker is a pastor of Aldersgate United Methodist Church in Grand Rapids, Michigan. A native of Muskegon, Michigan, she is a graduate of Albion College, Eastern Michigan University, and United Theological Seminary. She is an ordained elder in the West Michigan Conference of The United Methodist Church and has served as a district superintendent.

John Ross Thompson is pastor of The United Methodist Church in Grandville, Michigan. A native of Erie

County, Pennsylvania, he is a graduate of Pennsylvania State University, Drew University Theological School, and Pittsburgh Theological Seminary and is an ordained elder in the West Michigan Conference of The United Methodist Church. For twenty-eight years he served as a pastor in the Western Pennsylvania Conference.

Ellen Brubaker and John Ross Thompson are married to each other and are the parents of seven children and six grandchildren.

JOURNEY THROUGH THE BIBLE: COLOSSIANS, 1 THESSALONIANS, 2 THESSALONIANS, 1 TIMOTHY, 2 TIMOTHY, TITUS, PHILEMON, HEBREWS, JAMES, 1 PETER, 2 PETER, 1 JOHN, 2 JOHN, 3 JOHN, JUDE. LEADER'S GUIDE. An official resource for The United Methodist Church prepared by the General Board of Discipleship through Church School Publications and published by Cokesbury, The United Methodist Publishing House; 201 Eighth Avenue, South; P.O. Box 801; Nashville, TN 37202-0801. Printed in the United States of America. Copyright ©1995 by Cokesbury.

To order copies of this publication, call toll free 800-672-1789. Call Monday through Friday 7:00–6:30 Central Time; 5:00–4:30 Pacific Time; Saturday 9:00–5:00. TDD/TT: 800-227-4091. Use your Cokesbury account, American Express, Visa, Discover, or MasterCard.

For information on acquiring this resource in braille, call collect: Trinity Braille Ministry, 602-973-1415.

Cokesbury

EDITORIAL TEAM

Diana L. Hynson,
Editor

Linda H. Leach,
Assistant Editor

Linda O. Spicer,
Adult Section Assistant

DESIGN TEAM

Ed Wynne,
Layout Designer

Susan J. Scruggs,
Design Supervisor,
Cover Design

ADMINISTRATIVE STAFF

Neil M. Alexander,
Vice-President, Publishing

Duane A. Ewers,
Editor of Church School Publications

Gary L. Ball-Kilbourne,
Senior Editor of Adult Publications

04 – 10 9 8 7 6 5 4 3

THIS PUBLICATION IS PRINTED ON RECYCLED PAPER

CONTENTS

Volume 15: Colossians—Jude
by Ellen Brubaker and John Ross Thompson

$\mathcal{I}$NTRODUCTION TO THE SERIES

The leader's guides provided for use with JOURNEY THROUGH THE BIBLE make the following assumptions:
- adults learn in different ways:
  - —by reading
  - —by listening to speakers
  - —by working on projects
  - —by drama and roleplay
  - —by using their imaginations
  - —by expressing themselves creatively
  - —by teaching others
- the mix of persons in your group is different from that found in any other group.
- the length of the actual time you have for teaching in a session may vary from thirty minutes to ninety minutes.
- the physical place where your class meets is not exactly like the place where any other group or class meets.
- your teaching skills, experiences, and preferences are unlike anyone else's.

We encourage you to discover and develop the ways you can best use the information and learning ideas in this leader's guide with your particular class. To get started, we suggest you try following these steps:

1. Think and pray about your individual class members. Who are they? What are they like? Why are they involved in this particular Bible study class at this particular time in their lives? What seem to be their needs? How do you think they learn best?
2. Think and pray about your class members as a group. A group takes on a character that can be different from the particular characters of the individuals who make up that group. How do your class members interact? What do they enjoy doing together? What would help them become stronger as a group?
3. Keep in mind that you are teaching this class for the sake of the class members, in order to help them increase in their faithfulness as disciples of Jesus Christ. Teachers sometimes fall prey to the danger of teaching in ways that are easiest for themselves. The best teachers accept the discomfort of taking risks and stretching their teaching skills in order to focus on what will really help the class members learn and grow in their faith.
4. Read the chapter in the study book. Read the assigned Bible passages. Read the background Bible passages, if any. Work through the Dimension 1 questions in the study book. Make a list of any items you do not understand and need to research further using such tools as Bible dictionaries, concordances, Bible atlases, and com-

mentaries. In other words, do your homework. Be prepared with your own knowledge about the Bible passages being studied by your class.
5. Read the chapter's material in the leader's guide. You might want to begin with the "Additional Bible Helps," found at the *end* of each chapter. Then look at each learning idea in the "Learning Menu."
6. Spend some time with the "Learning Menu." Notice that the "Learning Menu" is organized around Dimensions 1, 2, and 3 in the study book. Recognizing that different adults and adult classes will learn best using different teaching/learning methods, in each of the three Dimensions you will find
   - —at least one learning idea that is primarily discussion-based;
   - —at least one learning idea that begins with a method other than discussion, but which may lead into discussion.

   Make notes about which learning ideas will work best given the unique makeup and setting of your class.
7. Decide on a lesson plan. Which learning ideas will you lead the class members through when? What materials will you need? What other preparations do you need to make? How long do you plan to spend on a particular learning idea?
8. Many experienced teachers have found that they do better if they plan more than they actually use during a class session. They also know that their class members may become frustrated if they try to do too much during a class session. In other words
   - —plan more than you can actually use. That way, you have back-up learning ideas in case something does not work well or something takes much less time than you thought.
   - —don't try to do everything listed in the "Learning Menu." We have intentionally offered you much more than you can use in one class session.
   - —be flexible while you teach. A good lesson plan is only a guide for your use as you teach people. Keep the focus on your class members, not your lesson plan.
9. After you teach, evaluate the class session. What worked well? What did not? What did you learn from your experience of teaching that will help you plan for the next class session?

May God's Spirit be upon you as you lead your class on their *Journey Through the Bible*!

Questions or comments? Call Curric-U-Phone 1-800-251-8591

2   JOURNEY THROUGH THE BIBLE

FULLNESS

**Colossians
1:15-20;
2:6-15**

LEARNING MENU

Remember that persons have different learning styles: visual, oral, sensory, and so forth. Activities that accompany each Dimension in the study book offer several ways of helping learners to experience growth through Bible study. Choose a variety of activities that will meet these learning styles. Be sure to select at least one activity from each of the three Dimensions.

Session Goal

The goal is to help the learner move through an encounter with Scripture to a personal experience with God's Word.

Dimension 1 activities relate to the questions asked in the study book. The questions explore the nature of God in Christ and our relationship to the fullness of Christ in us.

Dimension 2 further explores the nature of Christ and our understanding of Christ in us. Remember that understanding the nature of Christ is both affirmation and mystery. The members of the class will have different perceptions as they move through the activities. The object of the chapter is not to instill a set doctrine; rather it is to offer the experience of Christ in the heart of the learner.

The goal of Dimension 3 is to guide learners to understand the fullness of life in Christ. In contemporary life we speak of wholeness. The activities here are meant to connect us to the fullness of Christ in our lives today.

Dimension 1:
What Does the Bible Say?

(A) Explore the word *fullness.*

- Write on a chalkboard or large piece of paper these four words: *full, whole, complete, perfect.*
- Assign one of these four words to each person or each small group.
- Ask each person to think of himself or herself and describe the feeling of being full, feeling whole, having a sense of being complete, or of being perfect.
- Ask participants to find a personal, creative way of doing this. They might
—describe a time when they felt most like this word;
—give other words that better explain this feeling;
—explain what color comes to mind when they think of this word and why;

—describe places that make them feel like this word;

—talk about a person who comes to mind when they think of this word;

—reflect on what life might be like for them in the future if this word would better describe them then.

● Ask each person next to explain how those four key words describe or reveal the nature of God to them. Encourage them to think about each person of the Trinity: God the Creator, Jesus Christ, and the Holy Spirit.

TEACHING TIP

Remember that no sense of who God is should be criticized. Any description is by nature only an incomplete portrayal of the Divine; such descriptions are but a step toward a fuller understanding of what to human beings is not completely explainable. We all can learn from the perception another person has about God.

● Compare the feelings class members had about themselves with the words they used to describe God. Ask:

—In what ways are they similar?

—In what ways are they different?

● Discuss whether persons who are "in Christ" (as Paul wrote) can know the fullness of God in their lives. Ask:

—How does this compare with being complete and whole?

—Is it possible to be perfect through God's grace?

● Note the Colossians passages that discuss the fullness of God in Jesus Christ and in human beings. Discuss:

—What do they tell us about God's fullness in us? (Compare Colossians 1:19 and 2:9-10.)

—If God's fullness is in us through Christ, what difference does that make in how we live?

(B) Answer Dimension 1 questions.

● Invite students who have not already done so to write out their answers to the questions in their study books. Answers to these questions include the following:

1. In Colossians 1:15-20, descriptions of Jesus Christ that are similar to descriptions of God the Creator include phrases such as *the firstborn of all creation*; *creator of all things in heaven and on earth*; *head of the body*; *having first place in everything*; *having the fullness of God*; *having reconciled all things within himself.*

2. In Colossians 1:19, Paul tells us that "all the fullness of God" was in Christ, and in Colossians 2:9, he repeated the statement and added the word *bodily*. Christ was the *Incarnation* of God. God's fullness dwelt in Christ in bodily form.

3. Colossians 2:10 states to Christians that "You have come to fullness in [Christ]," but all of chapter 2 expands on that idea. Look for images of security (2:6-7); encouragement (2:1-5); direction (2:8, 2:16-23); and accomplishments of Christ on our behalf (2:11-15).

4. Colossians 2:13 notes that "God made you alive together with him" when God forgave all our trespasses or sins. Chapter 3 discusses more fully how Christians come alive in their new lives with Christ: the contrast of old life with new life (3:5-17) and instructions for ordering one's household (3:18–4:1), worship (4:2-4), and hospitality (4:5-6).

(C) Dig deeper into the Dimension 1 questions.

● Use the following questions as discussion starters.

—If the godly characteristics mentioned in Colossians 1 are true of the man known as Jesus of Nazareth, what does this say to persons who call Jesus only a good man and not similar to God?

—How do they change your view of Jesus?

—What are the implications of having God in the body of Jesus while he was on earth? What difference does that make to you?

—Since Paul is talking to the Christians in the city of Colossae, it is clear that the fullness of God that was in Christ could also come to other human beings. If that could happen in the first century, what does it say about those of us in this century?

—What makes it possible for human beings to have God's fullness, and how can you tell in the way they live that they are full of God?

—Describe a time when you have felt forgiven. Did that experience make you feel alive?

—How else might you describe it?

Dimension 2: What Does the Bible Mean?

(D) Answer the question, *Who is Jesus Christ?*

● Have someone read aloud Colossians 1:15-20. Ask a second person to read it again from another translation of the Bible.

● Then read several creeds from your hymnal. Pay attention to the affirmations of the nature of Jesus the Christ.

● Refer also to the list in "Who Is Christ?" in the study book, page 4.

● Using a chalkboard or large sheet of paper, ask the class to list words or phrases they associate with their understanding of Jesus. (For example: *healer, teacher, Savior, creator, friend, Son of God.*)

● Now go over the list, assigning either the label "divine" to those terms that seem related to Christ's divinity or "human" to those that reveal the humanity of Jesus.

● Ask the class to list words that they would assign to the

nature of God apart from their understanding of Jesus Christ. Discuss their choices.

● Then ask the class to think of words or phrases that they believe to be particular to Jesus. When they think of Jesus the Christ, they think of him in this way.

TEACHING TIP
You may need to assure class members that there remains mystery as to the presence of the divine/human in Christ. He is fully both. Yet we struggle to know what that means theologically and as we live as his disciples.

(E) Examine the nature of the Christian life.

● Ask class members to turn to the list of attributes in "The Nature of Christians" on page 5 of the study book.
● Ask them to work individually or in pairs to develop a reverse paraphrase of those attributes, that is, to write in their own words the opposite of what that attribute is or means. They can jot down notes in their books next to the list or use a separate piece of paper.
● After the paraphrases are complete, discuss these questions:
—What are some of the opposite characteristics you have identified?
—What feelings were evoked by having to look at an opposing characterization? For example, how did you feel thinking of "destroyers of fruit" (1:6) or "lives unworthy of God" (1:10)?
—Did looking at these attributes "from the underside" reveal any new insights about "the right side"?
—If so, what are they?
—Did examining what Christian attributes are not bring a greater sense of conviction as to what the attributes are? Give a reason for your response.

(F) Chart your path of Christian growth.

● Refer class members to "The Path to Christian Growth" on page 6 in the study book.
● Form three small groups and ask each group to take a quick look at the verses mentioned in the text. Group one will refer to Colossians 1 and 2; group two to Colossians 3, and group three to Colossians 4. (As time permits during the activity, encourage all participants to look at all the Scripture references.)
● For a few minutes only, ask class members to consider these questions. You do not need to discuss them.
—How do these words of advice affect you?
—Which ones seem like second nature to you?
—Which ones are more difficult for you?

—Which words of advice have you never considered?
● After a brief time of reflection, distribute paper and markers. Ask each person to chart out his or her own path of growth as a Christian.
● The chart can be a realistic picture; a timeline; an abstract, conceptual drawing; or some other visual representation. Suggest that the chart show diversions as well as "successes." (Remember, no person's path to God is a straight, smooth one!)
● Invite volunteers to describe their chart to the other members.

Dimension 3: What Does the Bible Mean to Us?

(G) Play the mirror game.

● Read through the information in "Jesus Christ, the Mirror Image of God" and "We Are a Mirror Image of Christ" on pages 7-9 in the study book.
● Ask for two volunteers to play the mirror game. The mirror game requires concentration and team work.
● The pair stands facing each other. Person One begins by slowly moving arms, hands, legs, head, and face. Person Two follows the movement as closely as possible, as if he or she were the mirror image of Person One.
● Person One at first should make the motions slowly and deliberately in order to help the partner get into the rhythm. As they continue, the pace can pick up.
● After a few moments, ask the pair to change roles so that Person Two leads the movement and Person One is the mirror image.
● If time allows, and the class is enjoying the game, invite another pair of volunteers to play the game.
● Take time to discuss the experience of the game. Ask:
—What was it like to lead?
—Was it a challenge to follow?
—How did one partner differ from another?
—What did it feel like to watch rather than to participate more actively?
—How does this game compare to mirroring the life of Christ?
—Is mirroring the life of Christ a game?
—When and how can mirroring the life of Christ be fun?
—When is it serious?

(H) Become "little Christs."

● Bring newspapers and magazines to class. Give class members time to browse through these, looking for evidence of lifestyles in contemporary society.
● Discuss the many options available to individuals and families in today's world.

—What pressure is brought to bear on our choices of ways to live?

—From where does the pressure come?

—How difficult is it to live a life consistent with our Christian faith?

● Plan a time together as a class when you can share in a film (videotape) that raises issues that relate to living faithfully. The following films on videotape raise such questions. They are not specifically religious, but they raise issues of faith and values: *Shadowlands*, 1993; *Schindler's List*, 1993; *The Mission*, 1986; *Days of Wine and Roses*, 1962; *A River Runs Through It*, 1992; *My Left Foot*, 1989; *The Trip to Bountiful*, 1985; *Places in the Heart*, 1984; *Norma Rae*, 1979.

TEACHING TIP

Preview any film that you are not familiar with, judging the appropriateness of the video for your class. Remember that your church or your conference must have an umbrella license to show copyrighted videos at the church, even in a nonprofit Christian education setting. To get information on licensing, call or write to Motion Picture Licensing Corporation, P.O. Box 66970, Los Angeles, CA 90066-6970; Tel. 800-462-8855; FAX 310-822-4440.

● Plan for a discussion time after you see the film. Ask the following questions:

—Which characters seemed to act in accordance with Christian traits? Give reasons for your answers.

—Which characters acted in ways contrary to Christian values? Give reasons for your answers.

—To which characters or situations did you relate best? Why?

—What issues of faith does the film raise?

—What challenges to Christian faith are there?

—How do the characters respond to a Christian concept of grace?

—What results from a life that fails to reflect the fullness of Christ?

(I) Tell stories about your window to divinity.

● Ask class members to review the comments by William Sloan Coffin in "A Window to Divinity" on page 10 of the study book.

● Invite anyone who wishes to tell a personal story about an occasion when the mystery of God became clearer or when God seemed particularly close. Do not push anyone to share.

● If the storyteller is willing to answer questions about his or her story, initiate a discussion.

TEACHING TIP

Some, perhaps most, of the class members will have had at least one experience of feeling particularly close to God. That moment, for example, may have been at a critical time in a crisis, a poignant time with a loved one, an occasion of new or deeper insight into an important theological or life issue. Suggest examples to help group participants focus their thinking and identify their special story.

(J) Consider the spiritual disciplines.

● Have each person write a definition of *wholeness* that reflects the fullness of Christ in us with regard to body, mind, and spirit. Or, review the insights from activity (A).

● Give the class some time to reflect in silence on their definitions.

● Ask:

—What does each person need in order to move toward greater wholeness in each area? (We often use the terms *body*, *mind*, and *spirit* to encompass the unity of our personhood.)

● Invite special guests who can be a resource on aspects of wholeness, such as a person who can speak on nutrition, exercise, and health care; or one who can help in stretching the mind throughout all of life's stages, such as persons trained in pastoral care and counseling.

● Develop a list of spiritual disciplines that would lead to development of a deeper spiritual life, including Bible study, prayer, contemplation and meditation, journaling, and so on. Remember that there are numerous ways to do each of these disciplines.

● Encourage each person to investigate the various ways each of those disciplines can be done and then to choose one of the disciplines as a devotional practice. If class members already regularly practice one or more of those disciplines, encourage them to experiment with a new method or a new discipline.

● Offer the class the idea of entering into a covenant in which each member would pray for the other members of the class every day. Such a covenant can be a source of Christian growth.

TEACHING TIP

The word *discipline* is not negative. With regard to the spiritual life, *discipline* means voluntarily developing habits through which we become more open to God's presence.

Closing Prayer

O God, who comes to us in Jesus the Christ, we pray that the fullness of your presence, complete in the life, death, and resurrection of your Son, may be in us. Forgive us when we fail to open ourselves to you. Encourage us as we become all you created us to be. Remember us always with your love. Amen.

Additional Bible Helps

The Theological Concepts of Colossians

Colossians presents a very complex theological argument (just in case you hadn't noticed!) that is not readily understood with a casual glance at the text. Paul uses imagery that made sense to an audience familiar with the gnostic and Christian images of "elemental spirits of the universe," the indwelling of the fullness of deity, "putting off the body of the flesh," "spiritual circumcision," regulations of "Do not handle, Do not taste, Do not touch" (2:8-21). Those images, many of which are in Colossians 2, are less than transparent to the reader today.

Elemental Spirits

You may recall from the Dimension 2 material throughout the study book that in the prevalent heresy of gnosticism, the world was considered dualistic. That means that there were sharp and opposing views of the world. What is material and earthly is bad, tainted, or evil; what is spiritual is good, pure, undefiled.

"Elemental spirits of the universe" (2:8) refers to the widespread Greco-Roman belief that the universe was made up of heavenly beings or powers that ruled the universe, separate from physical beings, who were subject to those "spirits." By addressing an audience with familiar cosmic images, the writer could establish a common vocabulary with his readers and thus form a basis for his argument.

Paul's argument uses this common language to his advantage by restating these cosmic images and beliefs in such a way that they defined or described the spiritual truth about Christ. Jesus Christ, the risen son of God, is a spirit. That spirit is God and coexists with God (in the beginning was the Word). That spirit became flesh, lived as a human, and is now united with God after the Crucifixion and Resurrection. Jesus Christ is *the* elemental spirit of the universe, not some undefined heavenly being entirely separate from the physical realm of the universe.

In its original connotation, the elemental spirits of the universe are distinct and separate from the physical world. In using this language to explain the role of Christ, Paul affirms the indissoluble union of the physical and spiritual realm. All the earth is God's; Christ is co-creator with God; persons are created as physical beings but in the image of the eternal God, thus bringing into physical creation that spark of the divine. The Savior himself took human form, illustrating in a powerful and dynamic way the union between physical and spiritual and stamping an indelible mark of spiritual goodness on the material creation.

Spiritual Circumcision

Circumcision was the special mark of covenant between God and all the Jewish people, even though it is a ritual only for males (Genesis 17:9-11). This is a rite of inclusion, mandated for Jewish male children and others in the Hebrew household (17:12-14). Many of Israel's neighbors practiced circumcision as well, but for Jews, this practice apparently served as a guard from evil. With this ancient understanding of the protective powers of the ritual, it is not difficult to make the theological leap that through this practice and symbolism of circumcision, God entered into a protective covenantal relationship with God's people.

Symbolically and theologically, circumcision of something, like the "uncircumcised of ear" (Jeremiah 6:10) or the "uncircumcised heart" (Leviticus 26:41) referred to receptivity to God's word and will. In Colossians the references to circumcision (Colossians 2:11-13) mean that persons entered a spiritual covenant with Christ, but without having the physical ritual that the Hebrews did.

Dying and Rising With Christ

The imagery of circumcision in Colossians 2 is mingled with baptismal images of dying and rising with Christ, and though these images are compatible, they can be confusing. In this chapter, Paul introduces the fullness of life in Christ by contrasting the immanence of Christ with the falsity of power of those elemental spirits of the universe. From the basis of the power of Christ, Paul establishes his readers in a covenantal relationship with Christ through a symbolic circumcision, which serves also as a metaphor for baptism imagery. Then he completes his argument on the identity and work of Christ by establishing what Christ has done on our behalf.

For us, Christ has died (crucifixion, buried in baptism) and has saved us from our sins (the results of our broken covenant or "uncircumcision"). By rising again, the destructive power of death ("dead in trespasses and the uncircumcision of your flesh") was forgiven and erased. God set aside our sin by "nailing it to the cross" and then "disarmed the rulers and authorities" (back to the elemental spirits of the universe again!), thus making "us alive together with him" when we were symbolically "raised with him through faith in the power of God" in our own baptism.

2 LIFE ON THE EDGE

1 Thessalonians 4:13-18; 2 Thessalonians 1:5-12

LEARNING MENU

Remember that persons have different learning styles: visual, oral, sensory, and so forth. Activities that accompany each Dimension in the study book offer several ways of helping learners to experience growth through Bible study. Choose a variety of activities that will meet these learning styles. Be sure to select at least one activity from each of the three Dimensions.

Session Goal

The goal of this session is to help group members better understand the issues that faced the Thessalonian congregation and to identify how those issues are like or unlike ones they face today.

Dimension 1:
What Does the Bible Say?

(A) Answer Dimension 1 questions from the study book.

1. Paul describes in 1 Thessalonians 4:13-18 what will happen to Christian believers when Christ comes. First, those who have already physically died will rise up (4:14, 16); and then those who are living will also be united with Christ (4:15, 17). Believers will meet Christ in the air.

2. Second Thessalonians 1:5-10 describes vengeance, punishment, and separation from God for those who do not know God and for those who do not obey the gospel. Note that the judgment comes from God and not from human beings. God's justice "will repay with affliction those who afflict" the believers (2 Thessalonians 1:6-7).

3. All of 2 Thessalonians is meant to prepare believers for the coming judgment of God. Believers should not be deceived; stand firm and hold fast to the traditions that they were taught; and keep away from believers who are living in idleness and not according to the tradition that they have received.

(B) Dig deeper into Dimension 1 questions.

● Ask class members the following questions:
—How do you feel about the resurrection of those you know who have died?
—How do you feel about yourself being united with Christ?
—If God will afflict those who cause affliction, will any of us escape God's punishment? If so, how?
—What distinction might be made between those who "do not know God" and those who do?
● Study 2 Thessalonians 1:11-12 and discuss the following question:
—What would life be like if Paul's prayer for Christians is answered?

8

(C) Roleplay the idea of judgment.

- Form small groups and ask class members to discuss times when they have experienced judgment. These experiences may range from minor traffic violations to family situations where injustice may have been done. If any class members have served on a jury, they will have a firsthand account to share.
- Each group should acquaint itself with one of these times of judgment and roleplay it for the large group. Ask each small group to describe for the whole class what character each person is playing. Let the dialogue of the roleplaying tell the story.
- Ask for a volunteer from outside the small group to play the part of the judge. Have the "judge" make a decision.
- Lead a discussion on the need for judgment. Ask:
—Do human beings exhibit any apparent weaknesses when they are making judgment? If so, what are they?
—How did it feel to be the person facing judgment?
—How did it feel to be the person asking for judgment?
—What was your motive? (justice, retribution, revenge?)
—What did you experience as the judge?
—Was the issue one that clearly violated generally accepted social or religious norms?
—If the issue was more complex, what did you have to consider before making a decision?
- Bring small groups together to discuss the roleplays. Compare the roleplay and answers to the previous questions with the message of 2 Thessalonians 1. Ask:
—Is there any relationship between the roleplay actions and decisions and this Scripture? Give a reason for your answer.
—How do you feel about God's judgment on your life?
—Is that judgment some future thing that doesn't mean anything now or is there more urgency?
—Does the anticipation of God's judgment make a difference in how you live now?
—If future judgment is not a primary motivator behind your beliefs and actions, what is? Why?

Dimension 2: What Does the Bible Mean?

(D) Check out the "troublemakers."

- Paul and Silas had an exciting trip through Philippi and Thessalonica. Read about it in Acts 16–17 and in "Paul's Visit to Thessalonica" on pages 12-14 in the study book.
- Look for this information:
—What people did Paul and/or Silas meet?
—What was the nature of their interaction? What happened?
—What effect did that encounter have on the person Paul and/or Silas met?

—What effect did that encounter have on the community?
—What consequences did the experience have for Paul and Silas?
—How did the missionary deal with it?
- When class members have gathered the information, divide into two groups (or pairs). Half will identify dangers; the other half, opportunities.
- Ask group members to pretend that they are one of the missionaries reflecting on the experiences of that journey.
- The persons looking for opportunities will go first. Either in the pair, or on behalf of the group, one person will mention a good thing or opportunity that arose from the visit.
- Using that as a starting place, the representative who is identifying dangers will counter the opportunity statement with "Yes, but . . ." and mention the danger.
- Continue identifying the dangers and opportunities for several minutes.
- Then discuss the total picture with two summary questions:
—Were the opportunities worth the dangers for Paul and company as Christian missionaries?
—Are your opportunities for ministry worth any dangers you may face? Give reasons for your answers.

(E) Let the Thessalonians debate.

- Read 1 Thessalonians 4:1-8 and review the section "A Life That Pleases God" in the study book, page 14.
- Before class prepare two copies of the role descriptions for Group 1 and two copies for Group 2.

Group 1. You are convinced that Christ is coming back very soon and will begin the new age. You believe Paul taught that your salvation is a gift from God. There are no conditions, and you can do nothing to earn more love from God in Christ. You are accepted as you are. This will be so when Christ returns.

As a group, you are all Gentile converts from a variety of ancient, pagan religions. Most of your religious background failed to connect daily living with the practice of faith. You know little of the Jewish grounding of faith in ethical living.

Right now, you see little value in working at trades in order to earn a living. There is so little time. Most of you are poor and have little or no education. This is as it has always been.

You see no reason why you should not expect more affluent members of the congregation to share what they have. After all, they won't be needing their wealth when Christ comes.

Group 2. You also believe that Christ will come soon. However, you understand that you are responsible for the way you live until that day. Paul modeled for you a way to conduct yourselves in daily life. He worked at his tentmaking trade while he was with you. He also taught you more of the ethical values that related to his former Jewish faith.

You have been leaders in the congregation because you have had the advantage of education and training. You believe that, while God gives freely the gift of grace, you will receive more of that grace if you harmonize daily life and practice with your faith. What you say and do does make a difference.

The more you model a holy life, the more you will be ready for life in the new reign that will be initiated when Christ returns. You believe in sharing of your abundance, but you also believe that the other group ought not to become dependent through laziness or poor habits.

- Tell the class that they will pretend that they are the Thessalonian congregation and will engage in a debate based on 1 Thessalonians 4:1-7.
- Divide the class into two sections so that each section contains two to eight people. If the class is large, divide the class into four smaller sections (two sections of "Group 1" and two sections of "Group 2"). Prepare two copies of each group's description. Ask each section to decide on a leader or spokesperson.
- Allow each group to read and discuss the content of its description card.
- Designate one person from each section to act as lead person in getting the discussion started.
- Set the scene. Say: "The congregation has been at worship. This means that they have shared a meal together as well as the celebration of the Eucharist, or Holy Communion. Group 1 brought nothing to share for the meal. Those in Group 2 have asked the congregation to remain after worship to discuss this growing dependence on the part of those in Group 1."
- Have the leader of Group 2 initiate the discussion by stating his or her group's complaint: "As leaders of the congregation, we want to remind the others that we need to integrate our faith and our practice. We want the members of Group 1 to do more to support themselves and the church. They may not have as much, but they can do their share."
- The leader of Group 1 should offer his or her group's point of view: "We don't have much in terms of material goods. While we enjoy the fellowship of the meals, we have other, maybe more important concerns. Christ is coming soon, and we want to be ready. We don't have time to fuss about who brought what to a meal."
- Let the discussion proceed as members of each group are encouraged to offer their opinions and the reasons for their attitudes.

TEACHING TIP

Remember that both the fun and value of roleplaying are in concentrating on staying in the assigned role. This allows persons to try out thoughts and behaviors that put them in another person's place.

- After ten minutes call time. Ask the groups to debrief. Share in the larger group:
—How did it feel to roleplay the Thessalonian congregation?
—What did you experience as a challenge from the "opposing" group?
—What main issues surfaced in the debate or conversation? What justification was provided for each issue?
—When varying viewpoints had validity, how did you reconcile those views with your group's point of view?
—What insight have you gained, if any, from participating in the roleplay?
—How did your role differ from your own reality?

(F) Think about and discuss the end times.

- Refer in the study book to "When Jesus Christ Returns" (page 15) and to "Watch and Wait" (page 17).
- Read 1 Thessalonians 5:1-6 aloud.
- Encourage participants to share their views on the end times. They may draw on scientific, theological, or experiential concepts.
- Ask and discuss the following questions:
—What recent events lead some people and groups to believe that the end of the world is coming soon? (For example, the bombing of the Federal Building in Oklahoma City in 1995 led once again to interest in end time predictions as people were confronted with the growing violence and hatred in the world.)
—How do we deal as limited human beings with the Scriptures, which remind us that the beginning and ending of creation as we know it is in God's hands? (1 Thessalonians 5:2 is a reminder. Jesus also cautioned the disciples just before the Ascension. See Acts 1:7.)
—How would we be different if we knew that the end would come exactly one year from now?
—How would your life be the same as it is now if you knew this were your last year?

TEACHING TIP

While none of us have experience with the second coming of Christ, we may have an inkling of what it is like to live on "short time." Some class members may have had to reorient their thinking and their lives when faced with a life-threatening illness or accident. Others may have watched a family member deal with a terminal disease, knowing that he or she had only months to live.

Be sensitive to these possibilities. If class members are willing, invite them to compare that experience with what they imagine about facing the end time.

(G) Contemplate life on the edge.

- Review the first paragraph in Dimension 3, page 16 in the study book.
- Provide paper, pencils, and colored markers of some kind for participants.
- Ask each person to reflect on each decade of his or her life. Ask each person to list the times or events when life seemed chaotic or on the edge.
- Invite anyone who wants to be more artistic to draw a life map or to decorate their list with images, icons, or pictures that illustrate those major life events.

TEACHING TIP

Most of our experience in church is quite verbal. We are often afraid to allow time for silence. Yet it is in silence that we often do the deepest reflection. Participants will come to value the times in class when the gift of silence is offered. The times of silence may grow as the class becomes more comfortable with quiet space.

- Ask students to pair up and for ten or fifteen minutes to share their reflections with one another. Allow each person the same amount of time. As they begin, remind them that discussing their personal experiences in this setting is voluntary. If they have written reflections that need to remain private, that is to be respected.
- Enter into a class discussion, using the following questions as guides if needed:
—What did you learn from the times of struggle?
—Was chaos or living on the edge necessarily bad? Give reasons for your answer.
—Some persons thrive on chaos or the excitement of living on the edge. Was the experience energizing in any way? How would you describe it?
—How was God present with you in those times?
—Did you experience a feeling of the absence of God? If so, what was it like?
—Are times of being on the edge necessary for growth of Christian character? Why or why not?

(H) Write a letter.

- Provide paper and pencils for the group.
- Ask students to write a letter to a young daughter, son, or friend who is away from family or loved ones for the first time and may be facing challenges.
- Write what you have attempted to model as you have sought to nurture them in the faith.
- Express your hopes for their continued growth in faith and

the habits they will need to cultivate for this growth to happen.
- Share with them what you have found to be the greatest sources of strength in growing as a Christian disciple.
- Mail the letter when you think the time is right.

(I) Sing (or say) songs of expectation.

- Read again the section "Songs of Expectation" on pages 16-17 in the study book.
- Distribute hymnals or song books that include these songs or others that reflect a yearning for the coming of God.
- If you have a good song leader in the group, invite him or her to lead in singing one or more of the songs. Otherwise, invite someone with oral interpretation skills to read aloud the lyrics.
- If you use one of the three songs mentioned in the study book, refer back to the commentary that accompanies the hymn or song.
- Ask these questions:
—How do these lyrics illustrate your concept of the end of time or the reign of God?
—What impact do the words have on you at a faith level? on an emotional level? on a rational level?

TEACHING TIP

If singing is not suitable, use a different creative medium. Use that medium to create symbols or other representations of the peace, justice, and joy that are suggested by the completion of life in the future reign of God in Christ. There may be resource persons who could be present to help with projects involving art, drama, or music.

Suggested media include murals or other art projects, poetry, creative movement or dance. One or more of these representations may fit in a service of worship or be suitable for display somewhere in the church.

Closing Prayer
Dear God, help us as believers to hold fast to the traditions that you have taught us. May we be steadfast and faithful. Encourage us to listen to you and to each other. May we enable one another by our attitudes of love and grace. In the name of Christ we pray. Amen.

Understanding the Day of the Lord
The Day of the Lord was a fearsome thing: destruction, devastation, ruin, pain, death—all falling on the hapless victims of God's wrath. The ancient Hebrews yearned for that day as vindication for the indignities and suffering Israel had endured at the hands of their captors.

Conquest and the Day of the Lord

Historically, Israel has had a checkered career of military conquests and defeats. The Old Testament is a record of the battles, victories, and losses of the people of God in the midst of often hostile neighbors. For centuries, the balance of power tilted back and forth among Israel and their neighbors surrounding Palestine: Moab, Philistia, and Syria, among others.

When Assyria, then Babylon, then Persia rose as military and political giants of the Middle East, tiny Israel entered a period of captivity and vassalage that continued for over a century. Assyria conquered the Northern Kingdom of Israel in 721 B.C. When Samaria, the capitol city, fell into the hands of Sargon II, it almost fell off the map. Israel, the Northern Kingdom, was gone, its citizens dispersed throughout the nation of Assyria as slaves and captives. Only the tiny Southern Kingdom of Judah, about half the geographic area of its counterpart in the north, was all that remained of what we know as the nation of Israel.

Judah's fortunes went the way of Samaria. Babylon had conquered Assyria by 609 and Judah became a vassal of Babylon. In turn, Babylon besieged and ultimately overcame the Hebrew resistance in Jerusalem. The first major Babylonian victory and deportation of the Hebrews occurred in 597 B.C., followed by another in 587. With all the major leaders and citizens in exile in a foreign land, the fate of Israel looked bleak.

In captivity, God's people faced not only a grave political crisis, but a theological one as well. Since Israel understood itself as a *theocracy*, a nation ruled by God, the first question of profound import was, Is our ruler, God, not powerful enough to stave off the power of these foreign deities? Has the God of our covenant abandoned us? When Israel turned to look at their corporate sin, they had to admit their own blame and deserving of punishment.

God had not abandoned them; they had abandoned God. But repentance brings renewed hope. In the midst of the bleakness and hopelessness of captivity, the prophetic voice warned Israel's oppressors of the day of the Lord. Yahweh is not a God to be mocked, destroyed, or ignored. Though the nations may have an upper hand, all would come to ruin on the horrible and glorious day when God would return to vindicate God's chosen people.

Israel was vindicated. With the rise of the nation of Persia, Babylon was conquered. Under the Persian king Cyrus, the Hebrews found a greater measure of freedom, even being allowed to return to their homeland from exile. But with freedom comes complacency, and with complacency comes further sin and corruption.

As Israel committed against their own citizens the sins that had been committed against them, the prophets again warned of the coming of the day of the Lord. This time, though, God's justice was not for Israel the nation or for the corrupt kings and leaders but for the common folk—those who suffered the oppression of the ones who were supposed to care for them. The day of the Lord would be no less terrible or terrifying. And more than that, it would be turned inside out with God's wrath consuming the so-called righteous leaders of the nation for their sins against their own people. Israel endured cycles of sin and repentance. Though the cataclysmic day did not occur, it was not forgotten.

In the Interim

In what we call the intertestamental period, roughly 200 B.C.–A.D. 70, Jews faced a tremendous period of persecution, most viciously at the hands of Antiochus IV Epiphanes. (Some of his grisly work is described in all its gruesome horror in 2 Maccabees.) Recalling the promise and hope of the day of the Lord was no doubt one tenet of belief in the developing notion of resurrection of the faithful dead. It is in 2 Maccabees that we see evidence of the hope for vindication after death, rather than before, as the day of the Lord would provide.

God Will Come

Israel's fortunes came and went. The new Christians, converts from Judaism, retained their understanding of the righteous God who protects the oppressed and who oppresses the unrighteous. With Israel's history of their own sin and the sin thrust upon them by their conquering neighbors, they knew that their status as the chosen nation did not protect them from God's judgment.

As the New Testament community grew, new converts from religions other than Judaism did not understand the image of a day of the Lord. They did understand the immediacy of their danger from oppressive rulers in Rome. They also understood the power and hope for their own salvation and eternal vindication through the crucifixion and resurrection of Christ. As their theology developed, the notion of the day of the Lord joined with the belief and hope in a final judgment and resurrection for the faithful. Further, they believed that following his ascension, Jesus Christ would come again. With the belief in the Second Coming, "the day of the Lord" has several layers of meaning.

At this stage, Paul and other writers of the epistles claim the image of the day of the Lord to resurrect the hope of vindication by God of Christians whose lives were lost or imperiled by persecution. Paul was aware of the concern in the Thessalonian congregation for those whose death occurred before the Second Coming. Would they be separated from the bliss of eternal life?

Paul, and in later writings Peter, claims the multifaceted concept of the day of the Lord to reassure his readers. Though no one knows (nor has ever known) when the Lord will come, he will come. On that fateful day, the righteous will be united with Christ in the kingdom of God. Throughout the history of the Jews, and later the Christians, God is in control. God through Christ will never be defeated, nor will the faithful. Whether in persecution or peace, Christians can be assured that God's judgment will be certain and just. When that terrible and wonderful day comes, it will be like no other.

3

1 Timothy 3:1-13; Titus 1:5-9

*L*EADERSHIP IN THE CHURCH

Remember that persons have different learning styles: visual, oral, sensory, and so forth. Activities that accompany each Dimension in the study book offer several ways of helping learners to experience growth through Bible study. Choose a variety of activities that will meet these learning styles. Be sure to select at least one activity from each of the three Dimensions.

Session Goals

One goal in this lesson is to better understand the conflict over sound doctrine in the early church. Even denominations today that carry a fairly widespread unanimity of biblical and theological belief experience conflict from time to time. By understanding more of the struggle in the early church, we are able to look in a new way at the foundational doctrines of our faith.

Another major topic in today's session is leadership for the church. It is important to choose at least one activity regarding doctrine and one that concentrates on leadership. Be sure to maintain an environment where a diversity of interpretation is welcome and where participants can listen to and learn from one another.

Dimension 1: What Does the Bible Say?

(A) Answer Dimension 1 questions from the study book.

1. The early church was developing a hierarchy of leadership as well as defending itself from the influence of heretical or "pagan" thought and behavior. Bishops, elders, and deacons were called upon to be persons above reproach in their personal lives and in every expression of their faith: responsible, faithful in marriage and in parenting, growing in and modeling the Christian faith, hospitable. He was likewise to abstain from any word or deed that could cast shame or doubt on the integrity of his faith.

2. In biblical times, women were considered property of their husbands, with few legal rights. Those who had no husbands had no standing in the community, since status depended on the man. The fact that women were mentioned in this listing of church leaders is an important affirmation of their heightened status in the early church, as compared to society outside the church.

3. Family management was extremely important within the Christian community. Numerous texts in the New Testament point out the new responsibilities of parents, wives,

husbands, and children. Most of those texts expect *mutual* respect, a departure from the typical Greco-Roman standard of total male dominance in the household. The male's responsibilities were primary, however, and men were expected to raise up children who were obedient and submissive. If men were ineffective household leaders, they were assumed to be ineffective as leaders in other areas.

4. Your class will undoubtedly differ on the most important responsibility of early church leaders, leading to a good discussion of leadership then and now.

(B) Dig deeper into the Dimension 1 questions.

- Have available commentaries for further research.
- For question 1, look primarily at 1 Timothy 3:1-13 and Titus 1:5-9. List the qualities that church leaders needed in the first century.
- Where a negative quality is mentioned, such as "quarrelsome" (1 Timothy 3:3), list an opposite quality such as "bridge builder" or "likeable." When your list is complete, think of the persons in your church who have those qualities.
- For question 2, search 1 and 2 Timothy and Titus for references to women (see 1 Timothy 3:11; 5:1-6, 9-16; 2 Timothy 1:5; Titus 2:3-5).
- Discuss these questions:
—What was the relationship of the women in each passage to men?
—What was her place in society?
—What rights or privileges did she appear to have?
—How do you think her role, relationship to men, and responsibilities compare to our society?
- For question 3 notice the references to marriage, family, and household in 1 Timothy 3:2, 4-5, 12 and Titus 1:6. An obvious test of responsibility and faithfulness for early church leaders was the way they lived out their family lives.
- Discuss these questions:
—How do these standards compare with the standards in your local church for persons in leadership?
—How would you state the essence of these standards in today's language?
—Do you think that the literal, word-for-word application of these standards is valid now? Give a reason for your answer.
- For question 4 notice the emphasis on setting a good example and communicating the faith both within and beyond the church.
- Read 1 Timothy 3:7, 13 and Titus 1:9.
- Discuss these questions:
—What does it mean today to have a good standing in the faith? in the church?
—What kinds of activities might make outsiders feel that church leaders have fallen "into disgrace and the snare of the devil"?
—In what ways do we tolerate that behavior? How do we work to correct it?

(C) Interview church leaders.

- Have class members decide who the most effective leaders are in your congregation. They should consider all persons who they believe provide leadership, not limiting themselves to those who hold particular offices in the church at this time.
- Schedule interviews with some of these leaders, being sure to include men, women, and youth across the racial, ethnic, and socioeconomic range of your church membership.
- The class could talk with them individually, have a panel come to speak with the class, or have individual class members speak to them privately using these or other questions:
—What qualities do leaders see in others that have encouraged them to become leaders themselves?
—What qualities do the leaders feel are most important today for those who lead the church?
—What qualities do the leaders believe God has given them that enable them to be effective leaders?
- After the interviews, summarize qualities that were repeated by various leaders. Compare them with the qualities in the biblical texts given for this session.
- Ask these questions and discuss various viewpoints:
—How are these qualities similar?
—What new qualities seem to be emerging?
—If you were talking with someone you did not know well who wanted to be a leader in your congregation, what qualities would you most be looking for?

Dimension 2: What Does the Bible Mean?

(D) Explore the question, *What is sound doctrine?*

- Read 1 Timothy 1:3-7.
- Review the material in "Church Leaders and Outside Influences" (pages 20-21) and "What?" (page 22) in the study book.
- There were pagan influences at work in the congregations. Discuss your understanding of what some of these were.
- Ask someone to look up the definition of the term *gnostic* in a Bible dictionary. Refer also to the article "Dangerous Life and Times" at the end of the study book.
- Discuss the following questions:
—What are the main doctrines of the Christian faith?
—How would you describe them in your own words?
—What are some influences today that challenge those doctrines?
—Do you think that requiring one "right" answer is the way to keep our doctrine "pure"? Give a reason for your answer.

(E) Explore the creeds.

- Quickly skim the section "Why?" on page 23 in the study book to remind yourself of why codified beliefs were necessary and what effect a rigid code might have.
- Take some time to learn and/or review some of the primary doctrinal standards of Christian faith.
- Get copies of several creeds. Try to include the Nicene Creed, the Apostles' Creed, and at least one or two more modern creeds, such as the Korean Creed, A Statement of Faith of the United Church of Canada, or A Modern Affirmation. There may be others in your tradition that would be helpful. These are often found in denominational hymnals or books of worship.
- Divide into small groups.
- Assign one creed to each group. Ask the group to outline the major statements of faith in each and prepare to report back to the large group.
- As each group reports to the larger group, look for similarities and differences in how the creeds state our Christian doctrine.
- Expand your study by reviewing the doctrinal statements of your denomination. Your pastor or a teacher who has studied these doctrinal standards may be a helpful resource.

TEACHING TIP

Remind the class that most creeds developed in a time of struggle over diverse interpretations of doctrine. There were often bitter battles going on. In several instances the result of the creed served as a means of excluding from the Christian community all who could not confess the entirety of the creed. A more positive purpose for the formation of creeds or statements of faith is to clarify the boundaries of theological understanding. One person said that creeds put sacred fences around belief. At their best the creeds help us focus our formation in the faith.

(F) Develop a new credal statement.

This activity is often done in confirmation classes. It can be a helpful exercise for participants to clarify their own faith.
- As a large group, reflect on the issues of faith in the midst of diverse interpretation of doctrine.
- In the creed include statements of faith about the nature of God, Jesus Christ, the Holy Spirit, the nature of humanity in relationship to God, the church and its mission. You may wish to add others.
- Share this creed with your congregation, perhaps in a service of worship.

Dimension 3: What Does the Bible Mean to Us?

(G) Take a survey of church influence.

We are told that the church today is a less powerful influence in the community and world than it was even as recently as the turn of the twentieth century. There were centuries when the church spoke for the state or existed side by side with secular authority.
- Locate in the library any reports from polls that measure the influence of the church today. (See George Gallup and others.) Share for a few moments from recent studies.
- Encourage the class to develop its own study.
- Develop a set of questions to ask of someone not involved in a church or faith community and plan how to do a survey.

TEACHING TIP

The purpose of the interview is to discover what influence the church has for those who are not a part of it. Emphasize that for the purposes of the interview, class members are only to seek information and are not to judge or persuade the nonchurched. We become better witnesses to the faith when we listen to persons and the needs they express.

Class members may need to be reminded that most studies tell us that half of the population of this country is unchurched. It should not be difficult to find someone to interview among one's co-workers, friends, or neighbors.

The interviewee needs to be told the purpose of the interview. The interviewer should listen to answers without questioning the opinion of the person being interviewed.

- Encourage class members individually to find unchurched persons who would be willing to be interviewed. Take notes that can later be shared with the class (with the person's permission).
- Develop your own list of questions, but consider questions similar to these:
—What does the church mean to you?
—What is your experience with the church?
—Do you read the church news in the paper or watch religious television?
—What do you learn from these?
—Do you believe that the church has any influence in your life despite the fact that you do not attend?
—If so, how?
—If the church has little or no influence in your life, why, do you think, is that so?
—Do you believe that religion or the church has some influence in the larger community of state, nation, and world?
—If so, how would you describe that influence?

—Should faith traditions have an influence in the life of the community? Why or why not?

—What religious leaders have had an influence on you, past and present?

—What, do you think, would happen in our society if there were no churches or faith traditions?

—What, in your opinion, could the church do to increase its influence in modern society and its emphasis on values?

● Discuss the results of the interviews in the class, keeping the identity of the persons interviewed confidential. The responses may help participants to explore creative ideas around the purpose and mission of your congregation.

● Share any helpful responses with the leadership of your congregation.

(H) Conduct an "attributes auction."

● Review "Today's Leaders" on page 26 of the study book.

● Read 1 Timothy 3:1-13 and identify in one or two words or phrases each of the attributes appropriate for church leadership. List these attributes on a large piece of paper and post it where everyone can see it.

● Explain that you are about to have an auction. Members will be bidding for the attributes that they think are most important and want their church leaders to have.

● Ask for one person to be the auctioneer and for another to record the winning bids.

● Tell group members that they each have the same number of dollars or points to invest in the auction (perhaps 1000).

● Each person should privately identify which of the listed attributes are the most important for church leaders and assign a maximum point or dollar value to bid for each attribute. Persons can bid more than they have originally allotted, but not more than their total points. The purpose of the initial estimate is to help persons keep track of how they want to allocate points to their most important attributes.

● Now start the auction, asking how much persons will bid for the first characteristic on the list. Continue through the list until all attributes have been auctioned or until persons are out of money or points.

● Following the auction, ask these questions:

—Which attributes have the highest priority?

—Did anyone invest all his or her points on a particular attribute? Which one? Ask why.

—Were any of the attributes ignored (and thereby considered unimportant)? If so, which one? Ask someone to discuss why.

—Which standards, when compared to their apparent importance to the early church, are still high priorities today?

—Which seem to apply to the early church but are not relevant for today?

—What leadership standards that were not mentioned in the Scripture are needed in church leaders today?

(I) Identify spiritual gifts.

● Invite class members to spend time in silent, prayerful reflection to consider the gifts that each has been given by God through the Holy Spirit. Ask each person to name for herself or himself one to three areas of giftedness.

TEACHING TIP

One of the challenges of growing in faith is to accept ourselves as persons loved by and gifted by a gracious God. People in the church have often been taught that true humility means not thinking well of oneself. This trait, however, stands in the way of developing the capacity to become what God calls us to be. The individual, the church, and the world are then deprived of the resources that each of us can bring. As Christians learn to name and nourish their talents, they often respond with a desire to share with others. Diversity of gifts, well-offered and well-used, builds the church.

During the activity, persons may be affirmed in hearing that others perceive similar gifts. It can also be affirming and challenging to hear others name gifts of which one is unaware.

● Form groups of three and allow five minutes for each person to mention perceptions of the gifts of the others in the group.

● Ask each person then to compare the perceptions shared by other group members with their own reflections of their spiritual gifts arrived at in the first portion of this activity.

● If there are persons who are new to the group, ask them to talk about the ways of serving in the church or world that bring them joy as well as ways of serving that do not bring them so much joy.

● Conclude with discussion of insights gained. Ask:

—What new avenues of service might be calling to you?

—Would you be willing to allow the church leadership to know of your openness to serve in new areas of ministry of the church? (Others may discover avenues of service beyond the local church. Emphasize that God's people serve in many places and in diverse ways.)

Closing Prayer

O God, you have given us many and wonderful gifts. Help each of us to hear you calling us into service through the unique talents that you have poured into our lives. Help us to nurture our gifts in holy ways. Encourage us to share our gifts, whether or not we become successful at everything we try to do. May we learn to risk new ventures in your name and for the sake of your people. In the name and spirit of Jesus the Christ, we pray. Amen.

Bishops, Elders, and Deacons in the Pastoral Epistles

The three primary terms used in 1 Timothy and Titus for church leaders are *bishop*, *elder*, and *deacon*. *A Theological Word Book of the Bible*, edited by Alan Richardson (Macmillan Company, 1950; pages 148-50), summarizes these three leaders as follows:

"We must now consider the ministers themselves and how they were organized in relation to the church and to one another. . . . We know what was the normal organization of the clergy throughout the ancient church from the [second century] onwards. A single BISHOP was the chief minister and ruler of the Christian people in a city or district. He alone was qualified to exercise *all* the functions of the ministry, and, in particular, he alone ordained others to the ministry by prayer and the laying on of hands. Associated with him, but without his power of ordaining others, were a body of PRESBYTERS (ELDERS) who as parishes multiplied became local parish priests, and again there were DEACONS, recognized as a third order, who assisted the bishop and his presbyters."

Who Are Deacons, Elders, and Bishops in The United Methodist Church?

The United Methodist Church has an order of clergy that closely models the biblical hierarchy. Deacons, elders, and bishops are all ordained ministers. Ordination, as a rite, is similar to baptism, a ritual that acknowledges publicly the church's intent to set apart men and women for public ministry.

Ordination

The United Methodist Book of Discipline—1992 describes ordination as "a public act of the Church which indicates acceptance by an individual of God's call to the upbuilding of the Church through the ministry of Word, Sacrament, and Order and acknowledgment and authentication of this call by the Christian community through prayers and the laying on of hands.

"It is a rite of the Church following New Testament usage as appears in the words of Paul to Timothy: 'I remind you to rekindle the gift of God that is within you through the laying on of my hands.' (2 Timothy 1:6).

"United Methodist tradition has entrusted persons in the ordained ministry with the responsibility for maintaining standards: for education and training and for examination and granting credentials to those who seek ordination. By the authorization of the clergy members of the Annual Conference, candidates are elected into the Annual Conference and are ordained by the bishop, who will use the historic language of the Holy Trinity: Father, Son, and Holy Spirit. . . .

"Ordination, thus, is that act by which the Church symbolizes a shared relationship between those ordained for sacramental and functional leadership and the Church community from which the person being ordained has come. The community is initiated by God, is given meaning and direction by Christ, and is sustained by the Holy Spirit. This relationship is a gift which comes through the grace of God in assurance of the ministry of Christ throughout the world" (¶ 432, pages 232-33).

The Ministry of Deacon

Persons currently set apart for ordained ministry are ordained twice; once as deacons, and after further education and/or supervision in an appointed church, charge, or other ministry, as elders. Deacons may be appointed to supervised ministries. They have the authority to conduct worship, preach, teach, perform wedding ceremonies in accordance with the laws of the state or province, and administer the sacraments in their appointed church or charge. At the invitation of an elder, they may assist in the sacraments elsewhere.

The Ministry of Elder

Elders are ordained following the completion of their education and their supervisory period under appointment. They meet the full requirements for the ministry of Word, Sacrament, and Order, which means elders can exercise the preaching and teaching offices of the church, all pastoral functions, the orderly administration of the sacraments without restriction, and the administrative work of a parish or other appointment. Elders, in conjunction with the local church leadership, oversee the general ministry of a local church or charge and are eligible to be elected as bishops.

The Ministry of Bishop

The ministry of bishops falls into three broad categories: spiritual and temporal leadership, presidential duties, and work with ordained and diaconal ministers and other commissioned personnel.

The spiritual and temporal leadership duties most closely parallel the duties of any elder, but they have the broader application within an annual conference, rather than a particular local church. The bishop is charged with the general oversight and coordination of ministry within one or more annual conferences.

Presidential duties include oversight for financial and programmatic operations of the annual conference, including any necessary coordination with boards and agencies within the annual conference. Bishops also appoint and supervise district superintendents, deacons, and elders; consecrate diaconal ministers; and commission deaconesses and missionaries.

Work with ordained and diaconal ministers includes making appointments within and between the annual conference(s) and overseeing the creation, consolidation, or closing of single and multiple-point churches or charges.

4

1 Timothy 4:11-16; 2 Timothy 2:1-7, 14-16

GUIDANCE FOR LIVING

Session Goal

As we continue the study of the Pastoral Letters to Timothy, we concentrate in this lesson on the need for continuing faith development. Timothy is young. If he is to witness and to lead in building the church, he must nurture his faith within. The goal is to understand more completely that faith comes often as a portion of our heritage from those who mentor us. It takes form in our lives, and we are called upon to share faith with others. The activities in the Dimensions of this chapter involve us in looking at our patterns of faith development and building upon those patterns for continued growth.

Dimension 1:
What Does the Bible Say?

(A) Answer Dimension 1 questions.

1. Timothy was called to active duty on behalf of the faith. A look particularly at 1 Timothy 4:11-16 notes numerous action words Paul used to instruct Timothy: "set . . . an example"; "public reading of scripture"; "exhorting"; "teaching"; "put . . . into practice"; "pay close attention"; "continue"; "in doing this."

Timothy was also to set a good example, being "strong in the grace" (2 Timothy 2:1), "a worker who has no need to be ashamed" (2:15). As you reflect on what Timothy was asked to do, notice how doing good things perpetuated Timothy's faithfulness.

2. Timothy was reminded several times that others were observing him and that his example was important both to Christians and to those outside the church. It was not enough to do right and be right. Timothy also had to avoid negative behavior, like quarreling or "profane chatter" (2:16) and "youthful passions" (2:22). Remembering that the first century church was a small minority in a hostile culture, vulnerable to criticism and persecution, the honorable actions of its leaders, such as Timothy, were crucial to its very survival.

3. In 2 Timothy 2:4-6 the soldier, athlete, and farmer are presented as persons who obeyed authority and worked hard. In contrast, those mentioned in 2 Timothy 3:1-8 were hard workers, but for the wrong goals. They were characterized as "treacherous" and "reckless" (3:4), persons to be avoided (3:5).

4. Second Timothy 2:15 urges Timothy to "present yourself to God as one approved by him," clearly indicating God's approval of one who is still young and relatively new to leadership in the church.

(B) Develop a portrait of Timothy.

● Assign each person in the class at least one chapter from 1 and 2 Timothy so that all ten chapters are assigned.
● Ask group members to skim their chapter and note all the characteristics, comments, suggestions, and inferences that cast light on Timothy's identity and character. Include references that describe his relationship to Paul and to his family. (The Scripture references in the shaded boxes in the study book will give you a hint as well.)
● After a few minutes of research, put together a composite picture of who you imagine Timothy to be.

> **TEACHING ALTERNATIVE**
>
> Add some visual creativity to this exercise by preparing before class several pictures of young men. Cut out pictures from magazines and paste a construction paper backing to them. Choose a variety of illustrations of men, both alone or with others, in various occupations or situations.
>
> When class members have done their Bible search, distribute the pictures. Ask each person in turn (or together) to use one or more of the pictures to describe Timothy. For example, a picture of a man in a business suit might reflect Timothy's sense of professionalism or the seriousness with which he takes his task, while a picture of a man with his family could characterize that Timothy also had a loving family.

Dimension 2:
What Does the Bible Mean?

(C) Find the false teachers.

Most of the information in the first section in Dimension 2 (pages 28-29 in the study book) introduces the theme of conflict in the early church and the need for strong countermeasures.

● Read this section in the study book. Form three teams and assign one of these chapters to each team: 1 Timothy 1, 6, and 2 Timothy 3.
● Ask teams to read their passage quickly and to identify the persons under criticism (if they are named) and what false teaching or conflictive behavior they are committing in the church.
● Discuss these questions:
—How are these false teachers described?
—What are they doing or accused of doing?
—What effect do they seem to have or are they expected to have in the faith community?
—How do they compare to the portrait of Timothy?
—If these false teachers were working in your church, what might be their effect?
—What can faithful persons do in the face of such disruption?

(D) Trace the ripples of faithful endeavor.

● In small groups, dig out the advice given to Timothy in 1 Timothy 4 and 2 Timothy 2 and 4.
● On a chalkboard or piece of poster paper, list those pieces of advice in a few key words, such as "avoid quarrels," "teach diligently," and so on.
● After listing key suggestions, collect opinions, reactions, and feelings regarding the usefulness and effectiveness of this advice.
● Then trace the ripples further to imagine what the church would be like if just one or two, then five or six, then all of these suggestions were carried out.
● When you are finished following the ripples, talk about new discoveries, insights, or dreams for the church.
● Use these questions to sustain the discussion:
—What seemed like the first or most important ripple effect for your church?
—What are the next ripples?
—What immediate changes did you see as you began to trace ripples?
—What short-range changes appeared?
—What long-range effects might be possible?
—How did you feel about the consequences you imagined if your church followed the suggestions for Christian belief and deportment?
—If you do not follow any of the ripples, what might be the consequences for your church?
—In what specific ways do you see you might need to change?
—In what ways are you already following the advice of Paul to Timothy?

(E) Decide who is a hero, a victim, and a fool.

Women are characterized in several apparently conflicting ways in the readings in this study. Sometimes women seem to be shoved to the sidelines as gossipy and foolish, easily led astray. In other cases, they are shown as pillars and exemplars of the faith.

- Skim the section "Behavior in the Household of God" (especially the last two paragraphs) on page 29 of the study book.
- Review the references that particularly mention women: 1 Timothy 2:8-15; 3:11 (women as deacons); 5:3-16; 2 Timothy 3:2-8; and Titus 2:3-5.
- Use a commentary and Bible dictionary to research the role of women and what these passages mean. Be sure to determine the historical and social context of each passage.
- Based on the research, decide in which of the Scripture references women seem as heroes, victims, or fools.
- Then discuss these questions:
—How do you feel about these characterizations in their historical context?
—What did this research teach you about the way women were regarded?
—If class members were divided in their opinions, what arguments persuaded them in their decisions?
—Do you think these characterizations are fair?
—Do they fit today's social-historical models for women? Give a reason for your answer.
—What do these characterizations say about the men of the time? Give reasons for your answers.

Dimension 3:
What Does the Bible Mean to Us?

(F) Grow in the faith.

Faith development is seen in spiritual disciplines or habits through which we open our lives to the presence of God in prayer, study of Scripture and other devotional literature, and faithful behavior of witness and service.

- Form small groups. Ask them to brainstorm ways of praying. Encourage them to draw on their own experi-

ences and habits of prayer.
- Discuss the results of the brainstorming in the large group.
- Use these questions to sustain the discussion:
—How can we grow in our lives of praising God and being thankful for God's grace and blessing?
—How can we best pray for our own needs?
—How can we expand our understanding and practice intercessory prayer (prayer for others)?
—How many ways to pray can you identify?
—What do you need to do to make time and space to listen to God?
- Then turn to the discipline of Scripture reading. Choose a passage such as 2 Timothy 7:9-22.
- Describe one method of Bible reading that immerses the reader in the story.
- Ask participants to read the passage, then reflect on these questions:
—What is the action?
—Who is involved?
—How do they each feel about what is going on?
—What might their motivations be?
—How do you feel about the persons and their reactions?
—What person do you relate to the most? Why?
—What person do you relate to the least? Why?
—What does the story mean to you personally?
—How do you see God at work here?
—How can you apply your insights from this story to your life today?

(G) Remember our saints.

- Give each person a few minutes to identify someone, living or dead, who has been a model or inspiration for them in the Christian faith.
- Invite them to tell their own stories about who that saint is and why.
- Ask class members to answer these questions for themselves and to include at least some of these answers when they tell their story:
—Who is the person? How is he or she related to me (if at all)?
—When did this saint live?
—What did he or she do that captivated my attention?
—Did this saint do or say something that was transformational for my life and faith? If so, what?
—Why did he or she have an impact on me and my faith?

(H) Identify real-life mentors.

- Have someone read 2 Timothy 1:3-7.
- Review "Learning From Others" on pages 31-32 in the study book.
- Ask the class to remember their saints.
- Activity (G) in session 2 invited participants to recall in periods of decades events of their lives that may have put them on the edge. Ask group members to recall those decades again and to remember the persons who were their mentors during that time.
- On a chalkboard or large piece of paper, post on the wall a definition or definitive words for *mentor* ("advisor, preparer, teacher, wise person"). Your dictionary or thesaurus may add other helpful words.
- Have class members write on the same chalkboard or large piece of paper the names of the persons who have nurtured their faith.
- Add the names of Lois and Eunice, Timothy's mother and grandmother, to the list.
- Talk about why these persons were important and effective mentors for you.

TEACHING TIP

Point out that a recent emphasis in the Protestant tradition has helped us once again to focus on our gratitude to those who have been with us in our faith development. The newest confirmation materials in some traditions encourage the pairing of confirmands with adults who can encourage them in their Christian growth. We celebrate the presence of mentoring persons on All Saints' Sunday. Sponsors or godparents, present at baptism, may serve in the same way as they nurture the spiritual growth of children and adults.

Remind class members that all of us teach something, whether directly or indirectly. When young people, new members, or anyone else hears about or sees what we do, even "behind the scenes," they learn something about us.

Young people, especially, are quick to notice when words and deeds do not match up, and they have little time or patience for religious hypocrisy.

(I) Consider becoming a mentor.

- Having read about and reflected on the models of faith in the Bible and in their own history, ask group members to identify quickly the key characteristics of effective mentors.
- Next, ask them to identify for themselves or for each other how many of those characteristics they have. (Persons may be reluctant to do this exercise for themselves. If so, do this in pairs.)
- Ask the following questions:
—What are the most important components of Christian faith that you hope you may pass on to others?
—Are you intentionally mentoring someone at present?
—If so, how do you carry out this ministry?
—What are you doing in the church that others may notice (even if you are not intentionally modeling anything)?
—What do your actions tell others about your faith?
—How can the church do more to build the process of mentoring children, youth, newcomers to the faith, and each other in a vital, growing faith commitment?

TEACHING TIP

In activity (H) of session 2 participants were asked to write a letter to a young person outlining behaviors they have attempted to model as important to the faith. If you did that activity, take some time to discuss the ideas that were in the letters.

(J) Identify other church saints.

- Distribute paper and pencils so that class members can do some journaling.
- Mentors offer one important ministry to the church, but not the only one. Spend some time in silence so that class members can read "The Ministry of All Christians" on pages 32-34 of the study book and reflect on it.
- Invite them in silence to write down some of their ideas of ways they can exercise their own ministries. This information does not have to be shared with anyone.

(K) Celebrate the ministry of all believers.

- Share with the group the nature of mentoring relationships in which class members may be presently engaged. Be sure to protect confidences. Reflect on the ministries each person offers.
- Now ask everyone to create a litany as an act of worship in the class. Let each person write the name of their saint, adding a sentence beginning, "Thank you for the gift of . . . ." Ask those who are willing to read them aloud.
- Consider collecting the litanies and using them for the church's celebration on All Saints' Sunday.
- Covenant with each other to continue praying for all those in ministry, those who are being served through those ministries, and the call of God to all Christians to pass on the faith to others.
- Conclude the class with a prayer for the church as it creates an environment in which all Christians may respond more and more to God's love and grace. The prayer might begin in silence; participants might add spoken prayers if they feel led to do so. The leader should begin the time of spoken prayer.

Closing Prayer

Gracious God, we are grateful for your church and its leaders. We pray that whether we are young in the faith or mature, we will lead according to the light that we have. Rid us of timidity and help us witness boldly on your behalf. Show us how to make our church a place of strength and peace for all: members and strangers alike. And lead us to such grace that none of your children are strangers to us, but friends and saints in the name of Christ. Amen.

Additional Bible Helps

More on Timothy

Timothy, referred to in 1 Corinthians 4:17 as Paul's "beloved and faithful child in the Lord" was a constant missionary partner of Paul.

"According to Paul's earlier Letters, Timothy was a colleague with Paul and Silvanus (Silas) in missions to the Thessalonians and the Corinthians. . . .The ministries of these three in Macedonia are also reported in Acts. . . . From both sources, we learn that shortly after leaving Thessalonica Paul's anxiety concerning the effects of persecution led him to send emissaries to encourage the Macedonian church in its faith. Paul, himself, was left alone in Athens. . . . From 1 Thessalonians 3:2-3 we learn that a special responsibility for ministry to the beleaguered Thessalonians was entrusted to Timothy, 'our brother and God's servant in the gospel of Christ.' When, with Silvanus (Silas), Timothy joined Paul in Corinth, he was the bearer of good news: the Thessalonians remained steadfast in 'faith and love,'" and they longed to see Paul.

"According to Acts, Paul's next major campaign in the East was located at Ephesus. . . . During the course of this ministry, several occasions arose in Paul's dealings with the Corinthian church that led him to send colleagues to act on his behalf. It is not clear that Timothy was the bearer of 1 Corinthians, or that a firm decision had been reached to send him to Corinth, but disturbances there made such a trip likely. . . . Some have surmised that Paul's plea concerning the church's reception of Timothy, should he come, indicates that the apostle had some doubts regarding his young colleague's effectiveness in a leadership capacity. . . . More likely, Paul feared that the Corinthians would complain that they merited the attention of the apostle in person, not the ministrations of an 'underling,' and that their anger would lead them to slight Timothy. A picture of Timothy as Paul's inexperienced, youthful protégé, intimidated by an aggressive opposition and needing the encouragement of his battle-hardened mentor, has sometimes been drawn from hortatory passages in 1 and 2 Timothy. . . . It is doubtful, however, that this image of Timothy is supported by references in the Letters generally acknowledged as authentically Pauline, and, in view of the probable origin and purpose of the pastoral Letters. . . , it is unlikely that the material describing 'Timothy' there is strictly biographical.

"In the prescript to 2 Corinthians, Timothy is again included, as Paul's 'brother' . . . It is therefore unlikely that Timothy's usefulness in dealing with the unruly Corinthians was at an end. . . .

"The later Letters of Paul continue to portray Timothy as a trusted associate and useful emissary of the apostle. . . . According to Phil. 2:19-24, Paul plans to send Timothy to Philippi and writes: 'I have no one like him, who will be genuinely anxious for your welfare. . . . Timothy's worth you know, how as a son with a father he has served with me in the gospel.'

"In none of Paul's Letters does he refer to his first meeting with Timothy. Acts 16:1-3 reports that Timothy was already 'a disciple' when Paul met him in Lystra. . . . According to Acts, Timothy's home life had been unlike that of the apostle. . . . Timothy's Jewish mother had married a Gentile, and their son had not been circumcised. This information would explain Paul's action in circumcising Timothy. . . after having so recently withstood the insistence of the Judaizers that Titus be circumcised. . . .

"While the pastoral Letters are of little help in reconstructing the personal history of Paul's younger colleague, there is no reason to doubt that their author knew the names of Timothy's mother and grandmother, Eunice and Lois."

(EXCERPTS AS SUBMITTED from HARPER'S BIBLE DICTIONARY by PAUL J. ACHTEMEIER, ET AL. Copyright © 1985 by The Society of Biblical Literature. Reprinted by permission of Harper Collins Publishers, Inc.)

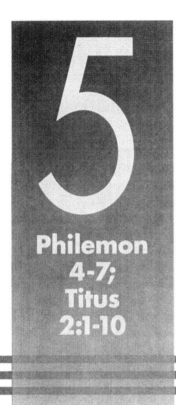

5

Philemon 4-7; Titus 2:1-10

HOSPITALITY AND OBEDIENCE

LEARNING MENU

Remember that persons have different learning styles: visual, oral, sensory, and so forth. Activities that accompany each Dimension in the study book offer several ways of helping learners to experience growth through Bible study. Choose a variety of activities that will meet these learning styles. Be sure to select at least one activity from each of the three Dimensions.

Session Goal

The goal in this lesson is to explore dimensions of Christian hospitality and obedience. When we are hospitable, we welcome others and place importance on their well-being. Christian hospitality is the Christlike way we are called to treat one another both within the church and in the world around us.

Obedience is behavior that comes from faith, with limits that one chooses because Christ is Lord of that person's life.

(A) Answer Dimension 1 questions.

● Urge students to answer the Dimension 1 questions before they come to class. Answers include the following:

1. The relationship between Paul and Philemon was close, marked by prayer (verse 4), knowledge of what Philemon was doing (5), good feelings, and a sense of being Christian brothers (7) as well as dear friends and coworkers (1).

2. The salutation to Apphia and Archippus (verse 2) from Paul and Timothy (1) and from other mutual acquaintances (23-24) indicate a warm relationship among Philemon and others in his house church and with Paul and his missionary coworkers. This is one letter that does not include any scoldings or admonitions to anyone (as in 1 Timothy 1:20 or 2 Timothy 4:14).

Philemon only was addressed in verses 4-21. Paul saw in him Christlike "love for all the saints" and "faith toward the Lord Jesus" (5). Paul commended him for "sharing of your faith" (6), for the "joy and encouragement from your love," and refreshment for the saints (7). It is obvious that

Paul saw Christlike virtues in the way these early Christians related to each other and to him.

3. Titus gave several reasons for concern about sound doctrine and behavior. He wanted to encourage younger persons (Titus 2:4, 6) and to bring credit to God's word (2:5) so that opponents would have nothing against them (2:8). He was hopeful that all Christians would live lives that honor God (2:10). He was concerned both about integrity within the church family and the image that the church had as a minority in a hostile culture.

4. Titus 2:1-10 is filled with references to controlled behavior, which shows itself in relationships with others both in the church and in personal lives. Those who are to live in submission to others are asked to do so because of their faith.

This passage is reflective of the authoritarian, tightly-controlled behavior expected in that day, both within the local culture and the highly-structured Roman empire. But it also reflects a different motive: everyone, including the authorities in the household and community, is to behave voluntarily in ways that glorify God.

(B) Confess times of disobedience.

- In small groups, have volunteers share times they have intentionally disobeyed. Some areas of disobedience may involve traffic laws; parental rules; doctor's instructions; guidelines for health; and matters of social justice, such as violating a law or policy that discriminates against someone on the basis of race, gender, or age.
- Discuss why this disobedience happened and both the good and bad elements of it. Focus also on the reasons why the persons chose disobedience.
- In the larger group, discuss the types of disobedience represented in the group.
- Draw a line on a chalkboard or poster paper, with one end being disobedience to all authority and the other end representing strict obedience in all things.
- Have group members determine where on the line they are in their lives and where each would like to be as a Christian.
- Compare responses to the kind of obedience and behavior that Paul seeks from Titus.

TEACHING TIP

Remind group members not to judge quickly the stance of other persons. Some disobey because of weakness or self-centeredness, which would be sin. Others choose disobedience because of a higher authority, such as an understanding of God's will that would reflect their Christian conviction. For example, how submissive should Christians be, as Paul suggests in Titus 2:5 and 2:9, if submission is not an "ornament to the doctrine of God" (2:10), but a cover for abuse?

Dimension 2:
What Does the Bible Mean?

(C) Recap the story of Philemon, Paul, and Onesimus.

- Read the Letter to Philemon and "Master and Slave Come to Christ" on pages 36-37 in the study book.
- Quickly go around the room and have group members retell the story. (Remember that the Bible does not tell us how the story ends.)
- Now collectively imagine an ending to the story based on what you know so far.
- Go around the room again and ask each person in turn to add one new detail to the story to make up a plausible ending.
- Do also activity (D) to get more details of the story. You will then return to your imagined ending.

(D) Discover who has the power.

- Read or review "The Hierarchy of the Household" on page 38 in the study book.
- Starting with the person who has the closest birthday after today's date, ask for any "aha" observations about the culture, context, or characters in the Letter to Philemon.
- On poster paper or a chalkboard, list these new learnings. They do not have to be in any kind of order.
- Now review your story with the imagined ending from the previous activity. Revise your story, if needed, based on your collective "aha" discoveries.
- Then discuss these questions:
—Who had the power? How extensive was it?
—What was the "worst case scenario" that Onesimus might have faced?
—What was his probable routine lot in life?
—What is the fullest implication of what Paul was asking Philemon?
—What might be your plausible ending to the story now?

(E) Investigate obedience and hospitality in Philemon and Titus.

- Look again at Titus 2–3 and at "Obedience and Hospitality" on pages 39-40 in the study book. Review Philemon, if necessary.
- Brainstorm and list the instructions for obedience and hospitality in these texts, especially Titus 3. Briefly discuss these instructions to be sure they are understandable.
- Choose one of the following cases to discuss.
- As you make suggestions about how to approach Phil or Tina, focus not only on what you would do or say, but what biblical or theological reasons you have.

—Phil is regarded as a loving and generous man by his family and friends. He is honest and hard-working and is held in high regard in his community and church. One of Phil's employees is on the brink of being fired because he will no longer put up with what is Phil's only blind spot: his constant hostility and insulting language toward persons of different racial and ethnic groups. What might you say to Phil? to his employee?

—Tina had some rocky times as a teenager, constantly out of the frying pan and into the fire. Her adult life is not much different, except that now she seems very restless. Tina seems to sense that something in her life is missing or is out of focus, but she can't name it. Years ago, she participated sporadically in church when her parents pressured her into going. When one of the pillars of the church confronted her as a teenager "at the brink of hell" for her wild behavior, Tina declared that door closed permanently. Tina wants to talk to you. What might you say to her?

(F) Explore issues of love and justice.

● Skim through "The Hierarchy of the Household" (page 38) and "A Call to Love and Justice" (page 39) in the study book.
● Pay particular attention to the situation of the slave as it was and as it compared to the rest of the household.
● Identify all the assumptions that had to be in place to maintain the system of slavery and the subservient role of persons in the household. For example, male heads of the household assumed they had the right to absolute authority or women had to assume they were unable or less able to manage a household.
● List these assumptions on poster paper or a chalkboard.
● Then identify current oppressive systems or unjust activities or behaviors that rely on deep-seated assumptions and name the assumptions that keep them afloat. Note how many assumptions are similar.
● One by one, challenge the assumptions with one or more issues of love and justice. Ask questions such as these to test and challenge the assumptions:
—How is this loving? How is it not loving?
—What would have to change to alter this assumption or this system?
—How hard would it be to effect a change? Who would have to participate?
—How do I perpetuate the system? How do I consciously or unconsciously support the underlying assumptions?
—In light of my Christian beliefs, what must I do or not do to transform the system?

Dimension 3: What Does the Bible Mean to Us?

(G) Investigate how obedience relates to power.

● Glance through "Corporate and Individual Obedience" and "Freedom and Slavery" on pages 40-41 in the study book.
● Ask class members to call out quickly relationships in which the sharing or balance of power is unequal; that is, one person or group in the relationship can require obedience from or has power over the other. This is the type of relationship between master and slave in the Roman system.
● List these relationships on a large sheet of paper or a chalkboard.
● On another sheet, list the ways in which each of these relationships is unequal, for example, economic, gender, age, race, status in the community, sexuality, national or cultural heritage.
● Divide into small groups. Ask each group to further examine one type of unequal relationship: women/men, rich/poor, young/old, dominant race/minority population; able-bodied/special needs.
● Direct the groups to discuss the ways in which the dominant group has power over the other in this category. Then ask:
—Why is this possible?
—What are the advantages to the dominant group?
—How is the dominant group able to continue its power over the other?
—How does it feel to be a part of the dominant group?
—How did the non-dominant group become so?
—What options are available to them for equalizing their power with the dominant group?
—How does it feel to be part of a group with another group holding power over you and your choices?
—If we are to take seriously the direction to welcome all equally as sisters and brothers in Christ, what must change for individual Christian disciples who are one in Christ? as the body of Christ, the church? as the church in the world?
● Ask each group to report to the class.

TEACHING TIP
In areas where all, or a majority, of your class members are in the power group, make certain that they seek also to understand these issues from the non-dominant groups' point of view. If possible, invite into the class a person or group of persons from such a non-dominant group to seek to understand their views. Use this important opportunity to broaden your own understanding, not to change the views of those who are not in the power group.

(H) Reflect on how to attack a problem.

The writer in Titus 1:10-16 attacks the problem of false teaching by attacking the false teachers. His disgust is transparent and obvious.

- Skim through these verses quickly and identify the ways and means the writer attacks false teaching and discuss the appropriateness of using the same approach to serious problems today.
- Use these questions to stimulate the discussion:
—Who is the writer talking about? What is their relationship to the readers of the letter?
—Who (or what) might be a comparable figure today?
—What means does the writer use to attack this issue?
—Do you think these means are justifiable for that era? for today?
—What is your favorite method for attacking a problem? Is it one that is compatible with your faith? that would bring glory to God?

(I) Discuss how your church welcomes others.

- Post in the room this verse of Scripture: "So if you consider me your partner, welcome him as you would welcome me" (Philemon 17).
- Using this verse as a springboard, conduct a churchwide scavenger hunt for the ways your church welcomes others.
- If possible, actually go around your church building. Invite a member of the evangelism committee and the pastor to go with you.
- Look for these sorts of things:
—signs that indicate times and places for church school classes and worship services;
—indicators of help available, such as nursery services;
—information about the mission of the church and its ongoing ministries;
—ways to identify members and guests to each other;
—policies and facilities that make the church and its program accessible (ramps, audio systems, large-print bulletins or curriculum resources, and so on).

(J) Develop a hospitality action plan.

- Consider the ways in which the parish seeks to continue the sense that all are important and welcome from their first visit to the church.
- Develop new ideas that would enhance the environment of hospitality in your congregation for members and guests.

- Then consider ways to extend the hospitality of your church beyond your own doors.
- Brainstorm the options available to you. Examples could include:
—working together in home repair or Habitat for Humanity.
—offering service to elderly members of your congregation and/or community.
—planning an occasion when you might go together to a long-term care facility and visit those who seldom receive visitors. This could become ongoing. The need in most communities is great.
—visiting or sending representatives to institutions for special needs persons, such as those who are mentally or physically challenged. One small church delegation visited a ward in a mental hospital every month, where they provided a birthday celebration for residents of the ward featuring those whose birthday was in that month. Others write regularly to persons in facilities for long-term care who receive no mail.
—considering the ways in which your parish deals with people in poverty. Is there a need to serve people who are homeless or hungry? Could the class serve in a hands-on way? There are many, many groups looking for volunteer help.
—considering the space available in your church. Could some of this space offer hospitality in new ways? There are needs in many communities for space for daycare

for infants and children, day programming for older adults, after-school care, substance abuse self-help groups, continued education, tutoring, language instruction, and others.

—considering involvement in Special Olympics, March of Dimes activities, or other community activities focused on persons with special needs. Choose an option that fits the time and talents of the class. A task force or small committee would need to work out the details and times for service. It is essential that the persons being served be aware, when possible, and give permission for the involvement of the class.

Closing Prayer

O welcoming God, you invite us into your presence. At your table we eat and are filled. The abundance of your hospitality overflows, and we are blessed. Help us to create with you tables of hospitality where all of your people share in the food and fellowship of your grace. Help us to go out to our city streets and our countryside to invite to the banquet those who thought they were not welcome. Amen!

Additional Bible Helps

Biblical Hospitality

Hospitality, in the ancient Near East, could be a matter of life and death. In an arid climate, finding hospitality meant gaining a needed respite from heat and access to water, food, protection, and certain comforts.

Probably one of the best known scriptural examples of biblical hospitality is in Genesis 18, when Abraham is approached by three strangers, sojourners through the desert. Unknown to Abraham these strangers are in actuality angels. But while Abraham is unaware of the special status of his guests, in terms of the expected hospitality, it doesn't matter. His obligations as host brought an intricate ritual of social responsibility.

The first stage of this ritual is in testing the stranger, who could in fact be an enemy. The host or other members of the community might question the newcomer to discover more about his reasons for travel and for passing through a certain area. He may be asked for letters of recommendation; he might even be asked to leave. But if the host discerned that the traveler would fit in comfortably with the community's norms, he was welcomed by the hospitable act of footwashing. Footwashing moved the traveler from the status of stranger to guest.

In the next stage, the new guest was afforded the protection of his host. In most ancient societies, the foreigner and alien had no rights or legal standing within the community. His host was thus obligated to protect him from harm at any cost. Modern values recoil at the willingness of Lot to give up his two virgin daughters to the hostile crowd in place of two of those same angels/travelers (Genesis 19). But as their

patron in a society that valued women less than men, Lot was following the custom of hospitality expected of him. (And he didn't have to give up his daughters after all.)

In addition to the patronage, both guest and host were obligated to fulfill their roles in ways that brought honor to each other. An infringement of hospitality to the guest was an affront to the host as well. Both host and guest could alienate the relationship by hostility or rivalry, by usurping the role of the other, by asking for what was not offered or refusing what was offered, by neglect, or by generally failing to demonstrate good will.

The result of failed or successful hospitality transformed the guest into either an enemy or a friend. When havens from the desert were a necessity in travel, one did not take lightly his responsibility as host, for he might be the guest later in need of a friend. Allowing a guest to become an enemy risked future reprisal. But the guest become friend would likely spread news of his host's gracious treatment and cement the basis for future encounters between the persons or their kinsfolk.

Hospitality in the Early New Testament Era

When Jesus sent his seventy disciples ahead of him (Luke 10) he expected them to be taken care of. The Epistles also assume that hospitality will be readily available (for example: 2 Timothy 1:15-18; Titus 1:5; Philemon 4-7).

With the added dimension of persecution of Christians, the need for protection was even greater. Since many believers had been driven from their homes, finding food and shelter from Christian "kin" was a means to economic and personal survival. The teachings of Paul about the fellowship of Christians as members of the same body no doubt supported the social expectations for loving one another in both practical and spiritual ways. The Letters to Timothy that describe the duties of church leaders mention hospitality as a key trait.

With the assumptions so strong for the show and demonstration of hospitality, the contrasting rejection of false teachers takes on an even more powerful impact. John comments with some spirit that false teachers will attempt to deceive. "Do not receive into the house or welcome anyone who comes to you and does not bring this teaching; for to welcome is to participate in the evil deeds of such a person" (2 John 10-11).

But not all strangers were enemies of the faith, and they deserved the care and hospitality of the community. "Beloved, you do faithfully whatever you do for the friends, even though they are strangers to you; they have testified to your love before the church. You will do well to send them on in a manner worthy of God; for they began their journey for the sake of Christ, accepting no support from nonbelievers. Therefore we ought to support such people, so that we may become co-workers with the truth" (3 John 5-8). Thus, strangers are transformed as friends and as friends of the faith.

6

Hebrews 1:1-4; 4:1-11

CHRIST IS OUR BRIDGE

LEARNING MENU

Remember that persons have different learning styles: visual, oral, sensory, and so forth. Activities that accompany each Dimension in the study book offer several ways of helping learners to experience growth through Bible study. Choose a variety of activities that will meet these learning styles. Be sure to select at least one activity from each of the three Dimensions.

Session Goal

The goal of this session is to explore the ministry of Christ as mediator, the bridge between God and human beings. You will also understand that we become separated from God and need the ministry of mediation. It is our need, not God's, that necessitates creating a bridge to God. This is something that we cannot do for ourselves. We must also consider how the barriers we erect separate us from God's unconditional love that is always available for us.

TEACHING TIP

Experts in human personality would teach us that we are complex beings when it comes to a sense of sin or conscience and a sense of self-worth. We learn what we choose to believe about ourselves from many sources. We also act on what we believe to be true about ourselves. What class members may say about a doctrine or belief may be different from the reality of a person's feelings or actions. Through study and discussion in the class, participants may reach new clarity on their own perceptions of faith. You, as leader, can help group members by asking them to compare what they believe about the Christian faith with their self-perception.

Dimension 1:
What Does the Bible Say?

(A) Answer Dimension 1 questions.

1. God has spoken in the past by prophets, but more recently by the Son of God, Jesus Christ (Hebrews 1:1-2). This community of faith also had circulating as their

Scripture some of what we regard as the Old Testament. The heavy reliance upon those Scriptures (mostly references to Psalms) by the writer of Hebrews indicates that God's revelation was apparent in the written word as well.

2. Hebrews 1:3-4 presents God's Son as having the favored position on the right hand of God, superior to the angels who are with God. Jesus Christ is also represented as the incarnation of God, sent to be like his "brothers and sisters" in every way (2:14-18).

The writer accords several roles to Jesus Christ—co-creator of the world (1:2-3); prophet and apostle after the model of Moses (3:1-2); partners with humankind in faith (3:14); and the great high priest who intercedes for and justifies a sinful world. While this role is introduced in 4:14–5:10, Jesus as high priest is a significant theme throughout the Letter to the Hebrews.

3. The reason given for persons not entering God's rest is unfaithfulness. First mentioned in a reference to Psalm 95:8-11, the faith community is compared to the early Jews who wandered, complaining and hardhearted in the wilderness (Hebrews 3:7-11). Just as those ancestors rebelled against God's word, so the legacy continued. Those who were rebellious or not unified in the faith, had the same opportunity to hear as everyone else, but chose not to listen (4:1-3). Their disobedience would keep them from God's rest (4:6, 11). The writer is clear that God's promises are available to all, but by our own choice, we may fail to receive the joy of God's rest.

4. Since God's rest is compared to the sabbath rest (4:9), it is a respite from work. However, it is also a reward for obedience, since those who disobey do not receive it.

TEACHING TIP

Although the answer to questions may be obvious to you as the leader, especially when you look at the verses highlighted in the chapter, your students may understand the questions differently. If group members give a different answer than you found in the Scripture, ask them for the verses that they used. In Dimension 1 questions, insist on a verse of Scripture for each answer, but be open to different points of view that can make an interesting discussion.

(B) Dig deeper into the Dimension 1 questions.

● Discuss these questions about the Dimension 1 exercise:
—How does God speak to the world today?
—In what ways has God spoken directly to you?
—Why is it important that Jesus Christ is better than angels?
—What other roles or characterizations of Jesus are important to you?
—How does it feel to know that we will receive God's rest?

(C) Who is Jesus Christ?

● Form four teams and distribute paper and pens. Assign to each team one of the first four chapters of Hebrews. Ask everyone to review "Christology" on pages 46-47 in the study book.

● Ask each team to skim through its chapter and to list as many images, roles, or characterizations of Jesus Christ as they can find. They should note anything that provides greater insight into who Jesus Christ is or what he does or has done.

● When group members have team lists complete, quickly compile the identifiers to make a master list on a piece of poster paper. Post the master list where everyone can see it.

● Ask all participants to rank for themselves the importance of each role or characterization for their own faith and spiritual growth. They can rewrite the list on their own paper in ranked order or just copy the master list and number the items accordingly.

TEACHING TIP

This activity does not mean to suggest that Jesus Christ is unimportant in any way or that it is up to us to decide that it is more important for Jesus Christ to be a healer than a teacher, for example. While every aspect of Jesus Christ is worthy, persons experience their own spiritual growth and insight in a variety of ways, some more powerful for them than others. This activity will help group members to consider the many roles of Jesus Christ, while identifying for themselves the particular ways Jesus' life and actions have touched their lives.

● Ask for volunteers to share their rankings. Discuss as a group why participants relate to Jesus Christ in the ways they indicated.

● If there is a high degree of uniformity among group members, look at the roles or characterizations that were the least considered and explore them. What is there to learn from the lesser-known or considered roles or characterizations of Jesus Christ?

● If there is a high degree of diversity, give persons a chance to explain their various experiences of Christ.

(D) "Visit" the Tabernacle or the Temple.

● Gather several Bible dictionaries, commentaries, picture books, atlases, or other resources that have information, especially pictures, of the Tabernacle (described in Exodus 36–40) and the Temples in Jerusalem. Be sure to check first for the pictures.

- Refer to "From Priestly Sacrifice" on page 47 in the study book.
- Ask class members to work individually or in small groups to research the Scripture (especially Exodus 36 and 38 for the Tabernacle and 1 Kings 6–8 for the first Temple) and the reference materials for a description of what the worship places looked like.
- Encourage participants to try to draw their own picture of the basic structures and to compare their drawings with the pictures they find.
- Identify each area in which the priests offered sacrifices and the special areas, such as the altar, the holy of holies, the ark, and so on.
- Discuss the research to make sure class members have at least a mental image of where the priests performed their ritual work.

(E) Study the New Testament concept of atonement.

In the next chapter, there will be a brief review of Israel's understanding of atonement in the sacrificial system and of the place of the priest in that system.

- Read "From Priestly Sacrifice" on page 47 in the study book as a very brief Old Testament background for this activity.
- Have the class divide into small groups, each with several resource books. Ask them to use the resources in creating a definition of the word *atonement* in the New Testament.
- When each group has done its research work, ask the class to make one comprehensive definition of *atonement*. Post the final definition where class members can see it.

TEACHING TIP

Arrange ahead of time to have ready several resources that contain a definition of *atonement*. These resources should include dictionaries or a thesaurus, Bible dictionaries, commentaries, or other theological resource. Your church library may have what you need. If not, a public library will be of help. Your pastor or other church staff may also have books that would help in a study/discussion of *atonement*. Be sure to include non-theological dictionaries in order to get a broad base of the meaning of the word and the way it is understood today.

(F) Reflect on Christ as our mediator.

- Assign Hebrews 1–2 (and, if you wish, select passages from 1 John 2–3). These passages indicate that Jesus

has been sent from God to engage our sinful condition with his own perfection.

- Review "To Atonement" on page 47 in the study book.

> "When he had made purification for sins, he sat down at the right hand of the Majesty on high" (Hebrews 1:3b).
>
> "Therefore he had to become like his brothers and sisters in every respect, so that he might be a merciful and faithful high priest in the service of God, to make a sacrifice of atonement for the sins of the people" (Hebrews 2:17).

- Using the following questions, discuss the role of Christ as the one who makes atonement for us. Let each person express what that means to him or her.
—Why do we need a mediator?
—How does Jesus mediate for us?
—Can there be other mediators with God on our behalf?
—If so, who would they be and what would they do? (Mention that some Christians understand that saints of the church may play the role of intercessors, which can be a form of mediation.)
—Does intercessory prayer have a place in atoning for sin and restoring a right relationship with God, others, and self? Give a reason for your answer.

(G) Take a "rest."

This Old Testament reading is a summary by Moses of the covenant God made giving the Israelites the land of Canaan and his warning to them that failure to keep God's commandments would defeat the covenant. Moses promised, however, that if the people kept God's statutes they would remain long in the land (Deuteronomy 4:40). In the language of Hebrews, they will inherit their rest.

- Ask half the class to review Hebrews 3–4 and the other half to look up Deuteronomy 4, especially verses 32–40.
- Then have the separate groups write several different headlines as if they are introducing news stories about the events to which the passages refer.
- If you have time, ask participants to jot down phrases as if they are outlining their news story.
- Bring the two groups together and talk about the headlines. Then ask:
—How do you understand the meanings of *rest*?
—What must the people of faith do to inherit that rest? Do you think those requirements are reasonable? doable? Why?
—What image of God do you have from your research?
—What action by Jesus Christ brings about this rest?
—What does that mean to you? How do you feel about it? Explain your responses.

Dimension 3: What Does the Bible Mean to Us?

(H) Discuss unconditional love.

- Share the following information with the class:

   There needs to be a balance in the Christian faith between the acknowledgment of the sin that separates us from God and the truth of God's love for us that is without condition. At times, the church puts more emphasis on one than the other.

   Individual Christians are a product of what they learn at an early age about human nature. This knowledge comes from the home, the church, and the world around them. Remind the class that the most basic doctrine of humanity is that God created all of life, including human life, and called it good. God created humanity to enter into a loving, grace-filled relationship with the Creator. This is the primary stance of God toward God's people.

   We break this relationship from time to time when we turn away from God and God's purpose, when we make ourselves and our will the center of life. This is sin or the state of being separated from God, others, and self. Even in our sinful state, God loves us and desires our return. This activity encourages the affirmation of our human condition. A modern term used to describe the attitude we internalize about ourselves is *self-esteem.*

- Divide into pairs and have partners talk to each other about the following experiences:
—aspects of my life where I have confidence (self-esteem is in good shape);
—places where self-esteem is low.
- When both partners have answered, ask them to discuss what would help each other with issues of self-esteem.
- Gather again as a whole class. Discuss ways in which the church has helped to build self-esteem for the class members, including past and present experience.
- Continue with ways the church or faith may have hindered self-esteem.

TEACHING TIP

Remind participants that discussing personal issues is completely voluntary and that what is mentioned should be held in total confidence.

If possible, invite the pastor or a pastoral counselor to help the class better understand issues around attitudes of self-worth. In addition to current church programs and policies, the class might consider ways in which the congregation could create a greater environment of positive self-worth for persons of all ages within the church, community, schools, or other neighborhood institutions.

(I) Scale the wall of separation.

Both Hebrews 3:12-14 and 4:1-11 refer to being hardened by sin. This same concept occurs in other places in Scripture. In the Old Testament, the heart of Pharaoh was hardened, as shown in his resistance to letting Israel leave Egypt (Exodus 7). Both Judas Iscariot's betrayal (Matthew 26:23) and Simon Peter's denial (Matthew 26:34) are known by Jesus before they happen.

- Refer participants to "Accepting the Gift" on pages 50-51 in the study book. Then consider these questions:
—How would you describe a heart that is hardened by sin?
—What evidence of hardness of heart do you see in today's world, in individuals, in the community, in national or international life?
—How does such hardness of heart create a wall between ourselves and God, ourselves and others, our present selves and the persons we want to become?
—Are we able to tear down these walls through our own effort? If so, how? If not, why not?

(J) Make journal entries.

Journaling can often be a way for some persons to understand at a deeper level what is happening. Such an activity can be started in a class session and encouraged beyond class time. Some participants may already have developed this spiritual habit.

- Ask participants to bring a notebook or paper that can serve as a journal.
- For the purpose of the theme of chapter 6, ask them to reflect on places in life where each seems stuck in ways that keep them separated from God, others, and self.
- Ask the following questions to begin the time of reflection:
—When did this begin?
—What has happened since?
—How have you attempted to scale the wall or attempt to get unstuck?
—Where is the resistance to change or healing?
—What needs to happen for healing to take place?
—Who could help you through this?
- Covenant to pray for each other as each seeks reconciliation.

(K) Pray about healing our wounds.

- Secure some copies of services of healing prayer, such as those in your hymnal or book of worship.
- Discuss the parts of the service that apply to spiritual wounds more than to physical wounds. Ask:
—Why do we need to be healed in spirit?
—How can such a service be a bridge that leads to new life and healing of mind and spirit?

Closing Prayer

Dear Jesus, you come to us in ways that are as new and fresh as each morning. When we draw closer to you, we know our great need for your presence. We confront the great wall between ourselves and those we love and between ourselves and God's love. You help us to tear down the walls of hostility; you become the bridge to the wholeness of our lives. You fill our thoughts, our words, and our deeds with your grace. Come to us as we study and grow in faith. Amen.

Additional Bible Helps

The Gracious Gift of God

Jesus Christ, superior to angels, the reflection of God's glory, and the faithful high priest in the service of God has effected for us for all time the gracious gift of salvation. The introductory chapters of Hebrews describe Jesus Christ as a preeminent and preexistent being who with God was the creator of the world. Further chapters identify Jesus Christ, God in the flesh, as the mediator between God and a sinful humankind.

In the lengthy discussion in Hebrews about the role of mediator, Jesus is shown in the figure of the great high priest (the agent who offers the sacrifice) and as the sacrifice itself. With this atoning gift of himself, Jesus Christ has abolished the need for all time for the sacrifice of life to wipe away the stain of sin. He was and is the complete atonement for the separation of humans from God. And all this is an act of radical grace.

Prevenient Grace

In the system of Jewish ritual, offering sacrifices (grain, fruit, or animal) was a central act. When the priest offered the gift, either as a burnt offering or otherwise, the gift (or its aroma when burned) was pleasing to God. Thus appeased, God was perceived as offering forgiveness or cleansing for whatever sin was being atoned. Hebrews tells us that Jesus Christ was the final sacrifice. God would never ask for another sacrifice of life because the most perfect life had already been offered: God's Son.

Hebrews tells us that Jesus Christ existed with God before humans were aware of him. In like manner, the grace of God existed before our awareness of it. And like the work of Christ, that grace is offered freely and without cost to all persons.

One way we understand the magnitude of that grace and the cost to God is by recognizing the prevenient manner of grace. God's grace goes before us, before our awareness of it, before our acceptance of it, before our desire to manipulate it, before our refusal of it. Regardless of how we regard (or ignore) God's grace, it is there. There is nothing in our power that we can do to change the presence of God's grace.

Justifying Grace

Once we are aware, and God's grace makes us aware, we may encounter that transformational moment when the reality of what God's love has done for us becomes personalized. We hit that point at which we can acknowledge that Christ died for *me*. Even when we know in our minds, that knowledge may not immediately penetrate our hearts.

This transformational event for us is a point of justification; we acknowledge and admit our sinful status before God and accept his gift of Jesus Christ as the one who mediates a right relationship between God and humans. Justification does not have to be encased in a dramatic conversion experience though. In fact, it is not so much an event as it is a relationship. This, too, is a gracious gift of God, done without merit on our part, and initiated not by our own efforts, but by God's prevenient grace.

Sanctifying Grace

Having been prepared by God's prevenient grace and saved by God's justifying grace, we live and mature in faith because of God's sanctifying grace. Jesus Christ in Hebrews is called the "pioneer and perfecter of our faith." Though Jesus Christ may have perfected the faith, those who live it each day must look forward to perfection, believing that it comes when we are finally united with God in the Kingdom.

Before we attain the Kingdom, we find ourselves in need of constant renewal, casting off the transgressions we commit against others, repenting of the actions and inactions that separate us from God and others, and seeking greater insight and deeper faith in the total love of God. God's constant forgiveness and guidance lead us through this growth to Christian maturity until we attain that rest promised to the faithful.

7

CHRIST INTERCEDES FOR US

LEARNING MENU

Remember that persons have different learning styles: visual, oral, sensory, and so forth. Activities that accompany each dimension in the study book offer several ways of helping learners to experience growth through Bible study. Choose a variety of activities that will meet these learning styles. Be sure to select at least one activity from each of the three Dimensions.

Session Goals

There are several goals for this session: to gain understanding of the role of priest in the original covenant with Abraham and Sarah; to explore further the meaning of Jesus in the role of high priest in light of the sacrificial system in Israel's worship; to move toward greater understanding of the place of covenant making in our growth in faith; and to affirm the call to the functions of priesthood for all Christians.

Dimension 1:
What Does the Bible Say?

(A) Answer the questions in Dimension 1.

1. According to Hebrews 4:15, Jesus is able to sympathize with us because he has been tested the same as we have been. Hebrews 5:2-3 refers to the role of any human high priest, saying that he must deal gently with persons in his care because he too is weak and needs to make sacrifices.

Unlike previous high priests, however, Jesus is without sin (4:15), although we know he was tempted (Luke 4:1-13). If the Temptation is to mean anything, we must be able to assume that Jesus could have sinned if he had chosen to.

These passages present Jesus as very human, understanding the human condition, but as one who did not yield to human weakness by sinning. In the words of the Nicene Creed, Jesus is "true God" and "truly human" at the same time, and thus can both empathize with us in our weakness and lift us to what is divine.

2. According to Hebrews 5:5, Jesus was chosen to be high priest by the Creator God, the one who in Psalm 2:7

said, "You are my Son, today I have begotten you," an affirmation similar to the voice from heaven at Jesus' baptism, "You are my Son, the Beloved; with you I am well pleased" (Luke 3:22). The author is familiar with the Psalms, for Hebrews 5:6, "You are a priest forever, according to the order of Melchizedek," is from Psalm 110:4.

3. We can move from useless lives to worship of a living God because of the blood of Jesus which, according to Hebrews 9:14, will "purify our conscience." This moving from death to life happens because Jesus as the high priest, using his own blood, provides the way, just as priests in Hebrew tradition used the blood of animals to bridge the gap between God and human beings.

4. Our inheritance, secured by Jesus as high priest, is eternity. Hebrews 9:15 makes it clear that Jesus mediates the new covenant (also called the "new testament"). We no longer need to use the blood of animals as in the first covenant (the "old testament"), because the blood of Jesus provides the way.

(B) Discuss what blood can do.

- Assign a class member, or invite a health professional such as a nurse or doctor, to discuss what blood is and its purpose within the body.
- List the various things that blood does, such as bringing nourishment and oxygen to all parts of the body and taking away waste materials. Then, in a parallel column, list the things that Christ's blood does for us, such as making us holy and purifying our conscience (see Hebrews 9:11-15).
- Compare the life-giving properties of human blood with the eternal life-giving inheritance that comes "with the death of Jesus."
- Recall, especially if class members express distaste about talking about blood, that in Holy Communion the juice or wine symbolizes the blood of Jesus, given for us for new life.

(C) Sing about the blood of Jesus.

A rich source for imagery about the blood of Jesus is a hymnal, especially the hymns related to Christ's death. These hymns provide an understanding of the blood sacrifice that links the Old Testament view of covenant with the new covenant we find in Jesus.

- Look up several of the following hymns in *The United Methodist Hymnal*:
- —"Nothing but the Blood" (362)
- —"There Is a Fountain Filled with Blood" (622)
- —"Alas! and Did My Savior Bleed" (294, 359)
- —"O Sacred Head, Now Wounded" (286)
- —"O Love Divine, What Hast Thou Done" (287)
- —" 'Tis Finished! The Messiah Dies" (282)
- —"Hail, Thou Once Despised Jesus" (325)

—"When I Survey the Wondrous Cross" (298, 299)
- Sing, say, or read the hymns. Then answer the following questions:
- —What is the theology of sacrifice in this hymn?
- —What images are used to convey the sacrifice of Jesus?
- —To what does the "lamb" refer? (It is not mentioned in every hymn.)
- —What effect does Jesus' sacrifice have?
- —How does the image and action of Jesus Christ affect you?

Dimension 2: What Does the Bible Mean?

(D) Who is dull in understanding?

In Hebrews 5:11–6:12 the writer of Hebrews sounds as if he is speaking sharply and critically to the readers of this letter. What is he or she really trying to accomplish here?
- Ask group members to review this passage and "Dull in Understanding?" on pages 53-54 in the study book.
- Individually or in small groups, have participants paraphrase the passage, keeping the same order, but stating in colloquial language what the writer is saying. If you want to get adventuresome, choose some widely known figures (real or fictional) and paraphrase as if you were that person. (For example, how would this passage sound from "Dirty Harry," Newt Gingrich, Hillary Clinton, the Lion King, a televangelist, Jane Marple, or Phil Donohue?
- Then discuss the following questions?
- —Is this comment a scolding or put-down? Give a reason for your answer.
- —Is this comment inspirational or confidence building? Give a reason for your answer.
- —How would you feel if you were one of the congregation to receive the letter originally?
- —What important message do you get from this comment?

(E) Investigate the question, *Why Melchizedek?*

- Together or in teams read Hebrews 4:14–5:10; 7:1-28; and 9:11-15. Refer also to Genesis 14.
- Briefly read over "Who Is This Melchizedek. . .?" and "The Meaning of Priesthood" on pages 54-55 in the study book.
- Discuss as a class or in small groups the following questions:
- —What is the significance of the Canaanite roots of the priest, Melchizedek?
- —How, do you think, was God at work in or through Melchizedek?

—The nature of the authority of Melchizedek is both divine and secular. Are there places in today's world where the leader possesses both divine and secular authority? How does this work? (This seems most true today in some of the largely Muslim countries of the Middle East in which *mullahs* or leaders have authority over both realms. This is not true of every country where Islam is dominant.)

—There are people today who prefer to mix the sacred and divine authorities. What are the results they advocate?

—What is the role of Jesus as high priest after the order of Melchizedek?

—What is the nature of the authority of Christ for you, for the church, and in the world?

(F) What is the meaning of *sacrifice*?

• Provide a variety of Bible dictionaries and topical concordances for a Bible scavenger hunt. Annotated or study Bibles would be quite helpful.

• Refer class members to "The Importance and Meaning of Sacrifice" on pages 55-56 in the study books.

• Form teams of at least two or three persons. Be sure that you have research resources for each team.

• Tell teams that they are to find out as much of the following information as they can within whatever time limit you set:

—the variety of offerings

—the significance of each offering

—how each was performed

—the roles of the priest and the people

—how priest and people interacted with each other

TEACHING TIP

Look at Leviticus 1–6 and 16 especially for information about types of offerings (burnt, grain, well-being, purification, and reparation) and instructions about the rituals associated with them. Look also for references to sin and guilt offerings and offerings of thanksgiving.

If you want to keep score and offer some kind of reward for a high score in this friendly competition, you might ask participants to decide what it will be.

• Following the scavenger hunt, ask group members to look at Hebrews 9–10 and discuss these questions:

—What is Jesus Christ's role as high priest?

—How does he fulfill the offering and sacrifice that you learned about from the Old Testament?

—What is the effect of that sacrificial offering for us and all humankind?

(G) Plan a field trip or invite a guest.

This would be a perfect time to invite a rabbi or Jewish layperson knowledgeable in Hebrew Scripture to visit the class. Equally significant would be a trip to a synagogue for worship and dialogue.

• Ask the rabbi to explain the sacrificial system of the Hebrew Scriptures (what we call the Old Testament) and how they interpret those Scriptures today. Be sure to tell him or her what you want and how long the presentation can be, allowing time for questions and answers.

OR

Attend a Roman Catholic or Orthodox mass or invite a priest to class.

• Ask the priest to outline the development of the priestly role in Christianity, including the role of Christ as high priest; the current trends in the priesthood today; and how all Christians can be priests to each other.

• Be sure to tell him what you want and how long the presentation can be, allowing time for questions and answers.

• If you plan also to do activity (J), see the Teaching Tip included in that activity.

(H) Make covenants.

The covenant made between God and Abraham and Sarah in Genesis 12 and 17 was a covenant in which God promised to be their God and to be with them, and they promised to walk with God in faithfulness. Essentially, it is a statement saying, "I will be your God and you will be my people." Later, there were signs of the ratification of the covenant, including circumcision.

• Summarize the stories about God's covenant with Abram (or Abraham) and Sarai (or Sarah) in Genesis.

• Discuss the making of covenants in today's world. Examples include covenants between individuals, within family life, in communities, between those who govern and the people governed, and between nations. For example, marriage is a covenant between two persons; baptism is a covenant among God, the church, and an individual or family.

• Discuss the following questions:

—Where do covenants exist?

—What is the nature of the covenants that are made?

—Remembering that the nature of a covenant is a promise between the involved parties, what promises are made in the covenants that you are discussing?

—Who are the parties on each side of the covenant?

—Are the covenants equal or unequal? That is, do the parties share equal power in making and keeping the promises? The covenant between God and God's people is not one of equal power and authority on both sides.

—Do we need covenants today? Why?

Dimension 3:
What Does the Bible Mean to Us?

(I) Explore the ministry of intercession.

- Read over "Intercession for Each Other" on pages 57-58 in the study book.
- Discuss the ways in which Hebrews 4–10 affirms the covenant we have with God.
- Afterward, talk about the ministries within your church that offer various kinds of intercession for the spiritual, physical, and emotional health of persons.

(J) Priesthood is for all believers.

Most Protestant clergy are referred to or addressed as "pastor," "preacher," "minister," "brother" or "sister"; some are called priests, and are referred to as "father." Regardless of the form of address, all ordained clergy fulfill certain broad functions in the life of the church: pastor (caregiver); prophet (preacher, protector and speaker of the biblical message, especially when it is difficult to hear); and priest (worship leader, celebrant of the sacrament, symbol-bearer for the congregation). *Priesthood* is a historical term that sums up all those roles. The "priesthood of all believers" refers to the general ministry to which all are called by virtue of baptism.

- Summarize the previous paragraph for the class and add information from "A Shared Priesthood" on pages 58-59 in the study book.
- Discuss in class the role of the priest in the life of the church, in the sacraments, and in other roles as a church authority.
- Outline on poster paper the functions of the priest in directing the spiritual lives of the people of the parish.
- Discuss the following questions, then share the fruit of your conversation with the pastor, staff, and leaders of the parish.
—How might the priesthood of all believers encourage all disciples to be willing to be priests for one another?
—In what ways could the church expand the significance of this ministry if all persons were willing to serve in a priestly role?
—Why do some people feel the need for the priest?
—How might we better support those being baptized and their families?

— How might we develop the need for people to confess at times their struggles with someone who will listen in confidentiality and pray with them as intercessors?

(K) Study covenant worship.

- Tying together the call in Hebrews 9:14 to move from "dead works to worship the living God" and Hebrews 8:13 about the new covenant, search various worship services that renew our covenants with God. Most denominational hymnals and worship books have covenant services. Many churches plan a covenant service at the beginning of the new year.
- Using one or more covenant services as a resource, particularly the "Covenant Renewal Service" used by John Wesley (*The United Methodist Book of Worship*, 288) discuss these questions:
—What does God promise to us in making a covenant with us?
—What promises or commitments do we make as our part of the covenant with God?
—How does a service of covenant serve as a reminder to us as we go about our lives?
- Encourage the class to develop a brief service of covenant to be shared in class or with the congregation. There may be resource persons in worship who can help the class in creating such a service.

Closing Prayer

O God, you came to your daughter Sarah and to your son Abraham and made a covenant with them, promising to be their God. They promised to be your faithful people. Help us to keep our promise of covenant faithfulness to you. Forgive us when we break our promises. Please be our strength as we seek to be more faithful to the promises we have made with you. In the name of Christ, who was perfect in obedience. Amen.

Additional Bible Helps

Jesus Christ as High Priest

The contributions of the Book of Hebrews, especially to our understanding of Christ's present ministry, are summarized by Merrill C. Tenney in *New Testament Survey (Revised)* (William B. Eerdmans Publishing Company, 1985):

"The greatest single value of the book of Hebrews is its teaching on the present ministry and priesthood of Christ. There are many references in the New Testament to his ascension and his place at the right hand of the Father, but with the exception of Romans 8:34 none of these explains what he is now doing. Hebrews, by its interpretation of the Messianic reference in Psalm 110:4, 'Jehovah hath sworn, and will not repent: Thou art a priest forever, after the order of Melchizedek,' has given a whole new ground of assurance to the believer in Christ. As the Aaronic priesthood by its sacrifices and intercession ministered to the Old Testament believer who obeyed the law, so Christ, in a fuller measure, though invisible, ministers now to those under grace. Those who witnessed the passing of the Jewish priesthood and felt that with it a divinely ordained system of salvation had vanished, must have been greatly reassured by the teaching that this man 'for ever hath his priesthood unchangeable' (Heb. 7:24).

"Hebrews is an excellent specimen of teaching in the early church. . . . It is an exposition of one theme, the new revelation of God, based on the passages in the Old Testament that contain the latent truth, and developed in orderly rhetorical fashion to a climax. Its use of quotations gives a good idea of the passages and the methods of interpretation that were used by the Christian teachers of the first century.

"Doctrinally Hebrews accords with the Pauline epistles, although it is not patterned according to their phraseology. Its theme, like that of Romans and Galatians, is salvation by faith in the sacrifice of Christ. The illustration of Abraham's faith is given more space in Hebrews than any other instance, thus bringing it into line with Paul's use of it . . . . Hebrews is a good witness to the growing independence of the Gentile church and to the enlargement of universal revelation that came through Christ.

"In its Christology, Hebrews adds much to the doctrine of the atonement, which it places in a covenantal relationship. This book explains the meaning of the new covenant more fully than did Jeremiah, whom it quotes (Heb. 8:8-12; Jer. 31:31-34), or than did Jesus himself. Hebrews connects the incarnation with the atonement (Heb. 2:14-17).

"In the study of the Old Testament Hebrews is an excellent guide to the meaning of typology and to an understanding of the lasting significance of the Levitical ritual. It does not purport to give a detailed exposition of all the features of the offerings and feasts, but its confirmation of their prophetic function in pointing forward to Christ is a valuable key for unlocking the treasures of the Old Testament. It is the best commentary available on these subjects.

"The most familiar passage in Hebrews is, of course, the eleventh chapter; it sketches the progress of faith by the use of Old Testament illustrations. Romans, taking the text from Habakkuk, explains the meaning of *just* and shows who is justified and how he is justified. Galatians shows what the life under grace really is, an exercise of spiritual liberty, and so expounds the idea of *live*. Hebrews demonstrates the meaning and progress of *faith*. By its warnings, by its exhortations, and by its gallery of examples it seeks to show what faith is, how it functions, and what results it achieves. These three books, Romans, Galatians, and Hebrews, form a trilogy explaining the heart and essence of the Christian life of faith."

8
Hebrews 11:1-7; 12:1-2, 12-15

THE MEANING OF FAITH

Session Goals

In this session you will consider the meaning of faith in scriptural tradition and revisit the influence of the community of faith through the saints or "cloud of witnesses."

Dimension 1:
What Does the Bible Say?

(A) Discuss the Dimension 1 questions.

1. Faith is concerned with the invisible, including
—things hoped for (Hebrews 11:1)
—things not seen (11:1)
—the invisible things from which the visible is made (11:3).

As such, faith deals with past, present, and future. The past includes those things we can no longer see or touch. The present includes "what is seen" (11:3), whose source is not evident. The future includes our hope for what is to come.

2. Hebrews 11:4-7 relates how Abel, Enoch, and Noah showed their faith by doing things that pleased God. It is obvious that each of them knew God.

—Both Cain and Abel offered acceptable sacrifices to God but for Abel's offering "the LORD had regard" (see Genesis 4:4). When Cain and his offering were rejected, Cain killed Abel. Abel's faith "still speaks" because God continues to hear the cry of those who are victimized (see Genesis 4:10).

—Enoch had found a way to please God ("he walked with God"). His righteousness was great, because he did not die as humans do. "He was no more, because God took him" (see Genesis 5:21-24).

—God had established a covenant of blessing with Adam and Eve, but when they sinned, God cursed the ground and the relationship of humans with other living creatures. When their sin spread throughout the earth, Noah was seen by God as the only righteous man on earth. God vowed to destroy what God had originally created and blessed. Through Noah, the only one who believed God's warnings about the future and who followed God's commands, God returned the blessing (see Genesis 6–9).

3. The "cloud of witnesses" in Hebrews 12:1 refers back

to Hebrews 11. Clouds seem so shapeless, with boundaries impossible to define; and they are often too numerous to count. Just so, the cloud of witnesses is a symbol of the countless numbers of persons of faith who surround us. Make certain you note that these verses refer not only to those persons listed by name, but also to the following:

—those who passed through the Red Sea (11:29);
—soldiers who encircled the walls of Jericho before they fell (11:30);
—the Old Testament prophets (11:32);
—women (11:35);
—those who have suffered torture, persecution, and death (11:36-38).

4. The promises of healing, peace, and holiness in Hebrews 12:12-14 come through the grace of God (12:15). It is God who provides these gifts, unconditionally lavishing on those who believe the blessings of faith. The writer affirmed these gifts in the blessing he offered to the recipients of this letter (13:20-21).

5. "The root of bitterness" (Hebrews 12:15) picks up an image used in Deuteronomy 29:18. The Deuteronomy passage is part of a long discourse by Moses to the people of Israel about, among other things, the dangers of secret apostasy and idolatry (worshiping other gods and religions).

The congregation of the Hebrews was also in danger from false teaching and being drawn away from God. The writer assured them that this root of bitterness is overcome by God's grace. The grace God, available to all as an undeserved gift, overcomes all bitterness that causes trouble.

(B) Explore assurance and faith.

● Form small groups and have class members discuss things about which they are absolutely certain.
● Tell them to meditate for a few moments on these things. Then ask them to share them with each other, making lists of the things about which they have deep assurance.

TEACHING TIP

Although this is a serious subject, permit groups to be humorous, since humor reveals deep feelings. For example, someone may say that she is certain that there will always be an offering whenever she is at church or that with modern medical advances, he is more certain of taxes than he is of death.

Other possibilities include their love for another person, another person's faithfulness to them, the sun rising in the morning and setting in the evening, the love God has for them, Jesus' gift of life through the Resurrection, and so on.

Some class members may feel that there is nothing certain in this world. Others can help by discussing how they know that some things are for certain. Remind them that the New Testament presents faith as a gift from God, not something that we can have simply by trying to believe.

● Compile the lists from the groups and post them.
● Discuss with the whole group which of these beliefs come from Christian faith and which come from their personal experience.
● Ask them to mark with an "F" those assurances that come from faith, and with an "E" those things that come from personal experience.
● Go through the list again, circling all of the items that are unseen.
● Discuss Hebrews 11:1-3, which discusses faith in what is not yet seen.
● Summarize the discussion by asking class members to write a new definition of faith. Make certain that they include in that definition some words describing whether faith can be seen or not.

Dimension 2: What Does the Bible Mean?

(C) And how difficult was it?

Many persons find living out their faith difficult. Some persons think it is difficult to share or express their faith to others; they are afraid they will offend someone else or embarrass themselves. The early Christians had much more serious difficulties.

● Review "Difficult Times" on pages 61-62 in the study book. (The article "Dangerous Life and Times" on pages 109-112 will also be quite illuminating.)
● If you want to dig deeper, bring several Bible dictionaries or books on early Christian history.
● Discuss the kinds of things the persecuted Christians had to deal with compared with the most serious challenges to our faith these days.
● Reflect on what insights you have gained from the comparison.

(D) Search the legacy of faith in Hebrews 11.

● Review "A Community of Faith" on pages 62-63 in the study book.
● Read together Hebrews 11. Ask someone to jot down every specific name mentioned as an example of faith. (Cain, for instance, is mentioned, but not as a faithful witness.) Group members may be willing to check or underline each name in their own Bibles.
● Divide into small groups. Assign to each group an equal number of names. Mix in the less familiar names with the familiar ones.
● Ask if anyone is up to the challenge of finding names or other specific information about the nameless persons mentioned in 11:35-38.

- Provide Bible dictionaries and study Bibles and ask each group to research the persons on their list, finding answers to these questions:
—Is this person male or female?
—What is this person's contribution to the faith?
—Did this person act with anyone else? If so, who? Was his or her contribution really a joint effort?
—How is that person's faith a testimony to you?
—What struggles did these persons face that you can relate to or have to face yourself?

(E) Search the legacy of faith throughout the Bible.

- Ask each participant to choose a character from Scripture who is for him or her a model of vital faith. The choice can be from the faith stories in Hebrews 11 or from anywhere in the Bible.
- Have each one share briefly why that person is for them a model of faith. If there is room, list each character on poster paper with one sentence that describes their faith.
- Post the sheets of paper in the room. Allow time for participants to read the sheets from the other groups.
- Gather again as a larger group and allow time for questions and discussion of any of the biblical characters listed.

(F) Celebrate the ultimate example of faith.

- Reread "The Ultimate Example of Faith" on pages 63-64 in the study book.
- Ask group members to read Hebrews 12:1-13 in which Jesus is described as the "pioneer and perfecter of our faith."
- Use a "powerball" approach to having group members tell what for them personally are the top one or two greatest events in Jesus' ministry (see the Teaching Tip).
- When everyone has had at least two turns to respond, stop the powerball and ask the group to reflect together on what they have said individually.

TEACHING TIP

A "powerball" can be a soft ball, such as a tennis ball, a soft rubber ball, a small hand towel tied in a knot, or two handkerchiefs tied together. The point is to have something soft with enough weight to be tossed from person to person.

In a powerball discussion, one person starts by answering the question (a great event) and then tossing the powerball to someone else, who answers and tosses the ball to a third person. Try to do this exercise quickly ("hot potato" is another name for this game).

Be sure to point out that the answers are opinions, not right or wrong research answers. Unique and duplicate answers are both acceptable.

(G) Let mutual love continue.

- Skim over "Making the Example One's Own" on page 64 in the study book.
- Then reread Hebrews 5:11–6:12 and compare it with 12:14–13:19.
- Discuss these questions:
—How is the tone of these two passages alike or different?
—What, do you think, was the impact of the overall message to the congregation of Hebrews?
—What impact do these passages have on you and how you live your faith?

Dimension 3: What Does the Bible Mean to Us?

(H) Remember the departed saints.

- Ask the group to skim through the introduction to Dimension 3 on page 65 in the study book.
- Then refer to the highlighted quotes from Julian of Norwich, Hannah Whitall Smith, and others that are printed throughout the session in the study book.
- Invite class members to choose one of the quotes for reflection and comment.
- Use these questions to sustain a discussion:
—What special insight to the faith does this person seem to have?
—What idea has especially captivated your interest? Why?
—How might one of these ideas or new insights transform your faith?

(I) Invite the living saints to discuss ministry with you.

- Review "A Contemporary Cloud of Witnesses" and "The Story Continues" on pages 65-67 in the study book.
- Remind the group that previous chapters have included the remembering of special saints who have shared their gifts of faith. Many of these beloved ones are now those whose earthly journey is finished. They are a part of the cloud of witnesses. Some of those who surround us with strength in faith are what we call living saints.
- Ask the group to name several living saints active in the ministry of the congregation, but not a part of the class.
- Plan a session when they can be invited to the class. (See the Teaching Tip.)
- Prepare discussion items with which you might begin, such as the following:
—Tell us some of your personal history. Where were you born? What was your childhood like? What faith experience did you have as a child? Were you part of the church?

—Will you tell us about any personal breakthroughs or struggles in faith experiences you have had?

—How did it feel to go through the times of pain and frustration?

—How did you get through it?

—Who was there to help?

—What did you learn?

—What legacy would you choose to leave in passing on traditions of faithfulness for individuals and for the church?

● End the time together with a brief worship, a hymn, a brief Scripture (Hebrews 12:1-2), and a time of joint prayer as appropriate.

TEACHING TIP

Guests should be extended a personal invitation by a member of the class. An artistic written invitation could be included. Be clear that you are asking these saints to come and to discuss in small groups something of their journey in the faith. Each person invited will be in a small group of three or four. The class will ask questions of the guest. The guest does not have to give a speech.

If refreshments are not a regular part of the class time, this would be an appropriate occasion to enjoy a time of fellowship and get acquainted with the guests over coffee, tea, and light snacks.

Write thank you notes to the guests afterward.

(J) Recall your stories of faith.

● Reread Hebrews 12:1-3, 12-15.
● Ask class members to take some time to reflect on their faith journey, including the people and events that have been key to their growth in faith.
● Encourage each participant to focus on one person, event, or experience that has had a major influence in his or faith development at a particular time. The stories of faith may be from personal experiences, from a tradition of faith passed down in the family, from engagement with the written word, from sensory experience (what one saw, heard, touched, the world of art or music), from dreams or visions, from a time of meditation.

TEACHING TIP

Leaders should encourage diversity in such an activity. There are no rights or wrongs. From people's stories, the reality of the person becomes known. Storytelling gets closer to the truth than staying on the level of the intellectual/thinking functions.

● Divide into pairs. Allow time for each person to share a personal faith story with the other.
● Gather again in the large group and discuss these questions:
—What have I learned from telling a story about my faith?
—What have I learned from listening to another's story?

(K) Make Scripture your own.

There is not as much emphasis on memorizing Scripture as there was at one time. Still memorization is meaningful if what one memorizes has content that one desires to recall in given moments. Hebrews 12:1-2 is a Scripture worth committing to memory.

● Post a copy of the passage on the wall. Take time to discuss the two verses and their meaning for class participants.
● Questions to consider might include the following:
—Who are the cloud of witnesses who surround us?
—What for you is the weight that must be laid aside in order to run the race?
—Discuss the process of preparation a runner goes through in order to be ready to run a race. How is the life of faith like that?
—In what ways is Jesus the pioneer and perfecter of our faith?
—Why did he set aside the joy and endure the cross?
—What was the shame of the cross?
—What does it mean that Jesus is at the right hand of God?
● Divide into pairs. Help one another to commit the passage to memory. It is best to take a little at a time. Short sentences or phrases may do. Repeat them over and over. Take turns reciting portions of the passage. Continue the process until both participants are sure of the flow of the passage.

TEACHING TIP

Some people are better at memorization than others. Some are better than they think they are. This activity should be fun and helpful; it is not intended to create anxiety. Consider looking ahead of time at the chapter on memorization in the book, *Teaching the Bible to Adults and Youth*, by Dick Murray (Abingdon Press, Nashville, 1993).

This process is something that can be extended beyond class time, if the class members desire. Have them ask someone at home to help.

Closing Prayer

God, you invite us to come to you in faith. You promise to be with us whether the days are full of joy or tinged with pain. You send to us those who are willing to share the strength of their faith with us as we journey. Make us more aware of the lessons you seek to teach us in the ordinary experiences of life. Help us always to understand that you are with us. In the name and spirit of Jesus, the Christ. Amen.

Additional Bible Helps

A Brief Who's Who of Hebrews 11

The list of luminaries of the faith in Hebrews 11 is impressive not only for the faith of each individual, but also for the weaknesses of that person as well. Some of the characters' lives are well-known, or they are developed more fully in the text of the session or in the study book; they will not be considered in this article. Turn your attention to some of the lesser-known figures of the faith: Gideon, Barak, and Jephthah. God uses the powerful and the weak to accomplish God's purposes.

Gideon (Judges 6–8)

Gideon was selected by God to deliver Israel from the oppression of the Midianites, who worshiped Baal. Midian's conquest of Israel was so complete that the people were hiding in caves and living in the mountains. Because of fear or oppression, some of the Israelites had erected altars to Baal.

God asked Gideon to pull down the idol of Baal and replace it with an altar to God. When Gideon was told to take men and attack the troops of Midian, who were numbered "as thick as locusts," with an army that God had whittled down from thirty-two thousand to three hundred, Gideon obeyed, and the Midianites were routed.

The conquest of God through the leadership of Gideon ushered in a generation of peace for Israel. But Gideon, even with the favor of God, asked three different times before battle for signs of assurance from God. Following the expulsion of Midian, Gideon fell to the temptation of idolatry himself, accepting a fortune in gold from the earrings taken as booty to make an elaborate priestly garment. Nevertheless, Gideon "died at a good old age."

Barak (Judges 4–5)

Deborah was the judge of Israel during their oppression by King Jabin of Canaan. On God's behalf, she summoned Barak to command the attack against Sisera, general of Jabin's army. Barak gathered the ten thousand troops against overwhelming numbers of Canaanites, but God "threw Sisera and all his chariots and all his army into a panic" (4:15). The entire army was slaughtered while Sisera ran away on foot.

Though Barak is remembered as the hero, the women of the story deserve mention. Barak insisted that he would not go into battle, even with the assurance that God would protect them, unless Deborah consented to go. She consented, but prophesied that the downfall of Sisera would be accomplished not by Barak, but by a woman.

When Sisera ran off, he sought refuge in the tent of Jael, wife of a neighboring king with whom Canaan had peaceful relations. She offered him a deadly hospitality. Sisera drank, then hid under a rug, asking Jael to stand guard and turn away anyone looking for him. While he slept, Jael killed him. With Sisera out of the way, the Israelites destroyed King Jabin and broke the rule of Canaan.

Jephthah (Judges 11–12)

Jephthah was the son of Gilead and a prostitute. Gilead and his wife bore and raised legitimate sons who drove Jephthah out of the family and denied him an inheritance. Jephthah coped by joining a gang, evidently a powerful one.

When the going got rough for Israel at the hands of the Ammonites, the elders of Gilead sought out Jephthah and implored him for help. They agreed with the witness of the Lord to make him not just a commander, but a tribal chief. Jephthah accepted and began what is the only record of diplomatic negotiations in the Book of Judges.

Jephthah may have been a bandit, but he knew his history, presenting a compelling argument about how the Lord and Israel had not wronged the Ammonites. But the king of Ammon was not persuaded. With Jephthah in command, God delivered a mighty victory over Ammon.

That victory was marred by a tragic loss. Jephthah, who tried to wheel and deal with the Ammonites, also tried it with God. He vowed to God that he would offer as a burnt offering whoever came first from his house to greet him following victory.

Perhaps Jephthah meant to say "whatever," rather than "whoever." Human sacrifice was considered an abomination, and it was not unusual for householders to have animals that could easily be used for a burnt offering. But the returning victor was greeted first by his only child, his daughter. Despite his horror and pain at what he had promised, Jephthah kept his word.

9

**James
1:22-27;
2:14-26**

HEARING AND DOING

Session Goal

This lesson's goal is to explore the holistic nature of the faith that begins with God's reaching out to us in grace and that leads to our response of love. It includes both being in Christ and doing the will of God. Stress that class participants may continue to develop the balance of the inward and outward living of the faith as they continue to grow in Christian commitment.

Dimension 1:
What Does the Bible Say?

(A) Answer and discuss Dimension 1 questions.

1. James 1:23-24 says that persons who look into a mirror and then go away forget what they look like when their image is no longer in front of them. Likewise, those who hear the word, but do not act on it, show by their inaction that it has made no difference in their lives. An image that is forgotten is useless. In the same way, a word heard but not acted upon is for naught.

2. Pure, undefiled religion, according to James 1:27, is to: "care for orphans and widows in their distress, and to keep oneself unstained by the world." Thus, purity has two dimensions, both active and passive: acting on one's convictions by doing deeds of compassion and avoiding all things that would make us impure.

3. James 2:16 does not condemn saying, "Go in peace; keep warm and eat your fill." Rather, it chastises Christians because, although we say these kind words, "yet [we] do not supply their bodily needs." There is nothing wrong with wishing another person well. We wrong that person when our words are empty and we do not act on them.

4. The demons believe in God—and shudder, according to James 2:19. Yet, they do not do good deeds. Belief that is only in words, even belief that causes our opponents to react emotionally (such as the demons that shudder), only goes so far. The author of James goes on in the next few verses to give illustrations of persons who not only believed but acted on their belief by doing what was right.

5. The prostitute Rahab mentioned in James 2:25 (and in Hebrews 11:31) found favor with God, not because of her prostitution, but because she welcomed God's messengers and protected them from danger. (See the story in Joshua 2, and note that she is listed as an ancestor of Jesus in Matthew 1:5.)

The point is that even those who are held in disrepute by the so-called good people of society can know what is right and follow God's way by acting on those beliefs. The walls of judgment that we build to classify people are not the same as God's judgment. Even those whom the church considers evil can be those through whom God's work is done.

(B) Consider how to do what you say you will do.

- Distribute index cards to class members.
- Have them write on the cards as many New Year's resolutions or promises to do something as they can remember having made in the last two years.
- Then, have them indicate whether they lived up to these resolutions or promises.
- Gather in small groups. Discuss whether most people live out in action what they really want to do.
- Invite group members to use personal examples, if they feel comfortable, to discuss the reasons why they or others succeed or falter in living out their commitments.

TEACHING TIP

It is easy to be critical of persons for not doing what they say they will do. It is enlightening to consider whether we live lives of action as well as good words, as James admonishes us. Class members who use a personal example of a commitment left undone make themselves vulnerable, even though everyone in the class has been there in some way. Be sure to keep the environment for discussion safe.

(C) Demonstrate how we show partiality.

- Quickly review "Showing Partiality" on page 71 of the study book.
- Ask everyone to read James 2:1-7.
- Recruit three or four volunteers to present this passage as a pantomime or a skit. Other group members will watch silently.
- When the presentation is complete, discuss these questions:
—What is the point (or points) of the passage?
—What does this passage tell you about the early church?
—What, do you think, is meant in verse 5: "Has not God chosen the poor in the world to be rich in faith and to be heirs of the kingdom"?
—Is this a justification for keeping the poor poor? Give a reason for your answer.
—What does this passage say to your church? to you personally?

(D) Visit with Abraham and Rahab.

- Read James 2:14-26. The author of James points out the active faith of two characters in this Scripture.
- Make a list of others in the Bible who acted out the faith in a particular way.
- List on a piece of poster paper or a chalkboard the name of each person and add a sentence that describes a faithful action. Some examples include Sarah, Joseph, Moses, Miriam, Deborah, David, various apostles, Mary the mother of Christ, Mary Magdalene, Paul, Lydia, Stephen, Dorcas, or others.
- Have reference materials available to research each character as necessary.
- Focus on what each of these persons did that showed their faith. Then discuss these questions:
—In the context of the epistle of James, what were the works by which these persons are remembered even to this day?
—What does "justification by works" mean? What does it mean to you? How might this be different from justification by grace?

(E) Work on taming the tongue.

- Look over the section "Taming the Tongue" on page 72 in the study book.
- Read James 3:1-12 and talk for a few minutes about what the passage means.

- Then choose one or more of the following case studies and answer the questions that follow the case.

Case Study 1

- You don't know Marcie very well, but she seems like a fun, upbeat person; complimentary and appreciative. You have both just come from a meeting at the lay leader's newly redecorated house. Marcie was effusive in her admiration of the renovations, but as you leave the driveway, she opens her conversation with, "Did you ever see such a horrible blend of color and design?"
—What comment comes to mind? What do you actually say to Marcie?
—What might be Marcie's motive for such a remark?
—How does this exchange make you feel?
—What comment does James 3 make or suggest about Marcie's behavior? about yours?

Case Study 2

- You and your spouse or date have gone to dinner with Ty and Michelle. During dinner, the subject of child-rearing comes up. The four of you each have your thoughts about how to do certain things, but Ty and Michelle seem to have the most divergent opinions. The general conversation has turned into a specific argument about the curfew Ty imposed on their teenager and which Michelle opposed. People at nearby tables are beginning to look your way.
—What do you do or say?
—How does this exchange make you feel?
—What comment does James 3 make or suggest about Ty and Michelle's behavior? about yours?

Case Study 3

- One of your elderly relatives lives with you and has gradually been slowing down, forgetting things, leaving appliances turned on. Since this relative doesn't feel very well, you hear a lot of complaining about aches and pains. A few moments ago you discovered that the tea kettle had been unattended on the hot stove long enough to be black and dry, just short of a fire, and *you* exploded. Now you see the look of hurt in your relative's eyes.
—What do you do or say now?
—How do you feel?
—Do you need to make amends? If so, why and how?
—What comment does James 3 make or suggest about your behavior?

(F) Examine consequences of envy, ambition, and judgment.

- Read James 4 and quickly skim "Envy and Ambition" and "Judging Others" on page 72 in the study book.
- First identify all the words or phrases in the passage that

trigger a powerful response, such as "you ask and do not receive, because you ask wrongly" (4:3).
- Talk about what response these loaded words and phrases may have elicited in the original audience and in you.
- Then look for the advice that offers a corrective or alternative to the trigger comments.
- Afterward discuss these questions:
—What does James tell us are causes of envy, ambition, and judgment?
—What ought we to do about them?
—What, do you think, did James mean in verse 7? in verse 8?
—How would you interpret verse 17?
—What does James mean by the "right thing"?
—What is the "right thing" for you?
—How do you know?

Dimension 3: What Does the Bible Mean to Us?

(G) What constitutes faith?

Debates can be competitive, but this activity is one that should be enjoyed. This activity will be set up as a debate, but will be judged as a fish bowl exercise instead. Teams of three persons each are sufficient.

- Ask group members to review the introductory paragraphs of Dimension 3 and the section "Faith Versus Works" on pages 73-74 in the study book.
- Set up two teams to debate the statement: *Faith alone constitutes Christian commitment.*
- Team 1 will debate the affirmative. This team will develop a plan to support the statement. During the debate, they will be expected to present evidence and convincing arguments, including biblical references, that all that God requires is faith.
- Team 2 will debate the negative. This team will gather to develop a plan to prove with evidence and argument, including biblical references, that faith alone is not enough; one must also show faith by good works.
- The rest of the class will observe the debate and develop criteria on which they will judge the debate. Some possible criteria would include:
—Is the evidence presented convincing?
—How well are the debaters prepared?
—Are the arguments logical?
—How sound is the biblical argument?
—Did the debaters stick to the topic?
—How well did they respond to the challenge from the other side?
Other criteria may be added.

- The form of the debate should be as follows:
  For Team 1 the first debater presents a portion of the case or argument. At the end of the time (3-4 minutes), this person will challenge the other team's position with a question that must be dealt with in rebuttal or refutation.
- The first debater from Team 2 presents a portion of that team's case. This person also asks a question that must be responded to by Team 1.
- The process continues in turn with the second member of each team, who attempts to win points for their team by effectively defending their side in answer to the challenge. The rebuttal time for each team is about 2-3 minutes.
- In round three, a third team member is given three minutes to make a summary statement that supports the argument and evidence presented by their side.
- During the discussion, the debaters should keep silent. Ask the observers:
—Which argument seemed more compelling? Why?
—What insights did the debate raise about faith and works?
—What new ideas or images do you have about the relationship of faith to works?
—If you decided that faith alone constitutes Christian commitment, what place does works have in faith?

(H) Walk the talk.

The following sixteenth century prayer about work is contained in *The United Methodist Hymnal*, 409:
"The things, good Lord, that we pray for, give us the grace to labor for. Amen."

In recent years, there has been a great deal written on the nature of work in a context that exceeds simply what we do for money. This discussion of the nature and purpose of work is appropriate for this chapter on a fuller understanding of the harmony of faith and works in Christian commitment.
- Define *work*. Use a thesaurus if you have one. Investigate work in the biblical era by using a dictionary or companion to the Bible. Look under headings such as, "trade," "vocation," "work," "labor," or "employment."
- If you can prepare before class, make index cards with some of the terms that might be used for work or labor.
- Hand out cards at the beginning of the class time or of this activity.
- Divide into pairs. Ask each pair to talk about their understanding of the meaning of work. This may come from heritage or culture of both past and present.
- Using the word on the card, ask each to consider the ways in which this word affects their present understanding. These questions may be used to initiate the conversation:

—How might the definition of work as a calling or as mission shed new light on the meaning of work?
—How is the definition of work broadened if work is seen as an art or a way of life?
—How can any kind of employment be viewed as Christian vocation?
- Ask the pairs to conclude their time together by talking with each other about their understanding of their present work. This may be work that includes pay or work that does not include pay.
- Gather again in the larger group. Continue the discussion by asking each person to tell in a few sentences their present concept of their own work.
- Discuss also the ways in which the Christian faith informs and nurtures work. Are there ways that the harmony of faith and works could be improved?

(I) Write letters of concern.

In this activity, class members will have the opportunity to put some issues of faith or conviction into action.

TEACHING TIP

This activity will highlight the fact that issues will elicit different feelings from class members. God's Holy Spirit leads committed Christian people to express themselves in different ways. Use these differences to affirm the view in James that we must act on what we believe, even if it differs from the view of another.

Plan ahead to have available the addresses of elected officials as well as the names and addresses of agencies, ministries, and programs that address the needs of the poor. These are usually available at government centers. Often the church office will keep these up-to-date.

Your group may need to do more "homework" to discover more information about those issues before contacting others about them. If so, you can plan to make this a longer-range activity.

Some persons may doubt that writing letters will make a difference. Remind them that such activity has a cumulative effect on politicians and on institutions that serve the public. Such an effect over time can make a difference.

- Review "The Righteous Life" and "Regard for the Poor" on page 74 in the study book and James 5.
- Brainstorm for issues that affect the poor in or around your community. Identify what the needs are and what programs or ministries are in place to meet those needs. What are the root causes of the needs in your area or in the wider community?
- Distribute paper, envelopes, and stamps for individual letters or postcards. You might write a group letter instead.

- Begin with a time of discussion as to why we are called to take an active part in life around us.
- If you have discussed the issues thoroughly enough to take a stand or to make recommendations, write letters to appropriate persons, agencies, or institutions in your area. State your issue, give some background on your church affiliation and the church's stance, and politely state your requests for action.
- You may find that your own church needs to pay more attention to these issues. If so, survey the group for the commitments they are prepared to make and address your letter of concern to the administrative board, council on ministries, or appropriate ministry group.
- As an alternative, you may decide to offer your own services or commitment to ministry with community groups already in place to serve the poor. In this case, your letters would be offers of help rather than requests for change or action.
- Gather the letters and mail them. Some may wish to participate, but not want to share their point of view with others. Be sure you have permission to mail the letters.

Closing Devotional
- Read James 1:22-27.
- Sing or read the hymn, "Sent Forth by God's Blessing" (*The United Methodist Hymnal*, 664). Ask the class to pay close attention to the words, even if they are singing the hymn.
- Pray together:
  Great God of love, your son took a towel and basin and washed the feet of the disciples. He called us to minister in his name by feeding the hungry, giving water to the thirsty, and visiting the sick and those in prison. He said that we would teach and heal in his name. Give us the courage to respond to your love for us by actively loving your people and your world. In the name of the Christ who washes feet. Amen.

Additional Bible Helps

Faith as Right Thinking and as Right Living
The need for the Book of James in the first century, and in our time, is explained in *An Introduction to the Bible*, by James R. Beasley, Clyde E. Fant, E. Earl Joiner, Donald W. Musser, and Mitchell G. Reddish (Abingdon Press, 1991; pages 454-55) under the heading "Faith: Right Thinking or Right Living?"

"One of the distinctive shifts from the writings of Paul to the later New Testament writings concerns the meaning of faith. For Paul, faith is the absolute committal of the person to God, specifically to God's act in Christ as proclaimed in the kerygma [preaching]. It is also an absolute committal to God's grace, and it cannot be obtained by works (obedience to the Law; good deeds). Many passages in Romans (3:20-25; 9:30-32; 10:4-6; and others) are emphatic at this point, and the entire book of Galatians opposes the idea that faith must be supplemented by works of the Law for a person to stand justified before God. But it is apparent from the later New Testament writings that faith, at least in some circles, had come to mean an orthodoxy of ideas, a mental assent to a set of propositions. The book of James was written to counter just such a perversion of Pauline thought. . . .

"Is the thought of James in contradiction with that of Paul? James places considerable emphasis on deeds of compassion, particularly toward the poor (2:14-26) and orphans and widows (1:27). He also opposes favoritism toward the rich and discrimination toward the poor (2:1-7). These are the kinds of 'works' James wants Christians to practice. He says that 'faith without works is dead,' and he rebukes Christians who see someone 'ill-clad and in lack of daily food' and 'says to them, "Go in peace, be warmed and filled," without giving them the things needed for the body.' He asks, 'what does it profit?' (2:14-17). 'For as the body apart from the spirit is dead, so faith apart from works is dead' (2:26).

"When Paul speaks against the need for works, he is referring to such 'works of the Law' as circumcision and sacrifices. He would agree that real faith results in works of compassion, 'faith working through love' (Galatians 5:6). Paul's emphasis is on the faith-relationship required for right standing before God; James's emphasis is on the faith-actions required of living faith in contrast to dead faith.

"The book of James is clearly a manual of Christian conduct, much of it like the book of Proverbs. It treats true wisdom for Christians (1:5; 3:17) just as Hebrew Wisdom literature urged God's wisdom for Israel. Its use of hortatory admonitions, urging action on Christians, mark it as a sermon-treatise rather than a letter. As such, it continues to remind the church that belief and behavior, doctrine and ethics, belong together."

10

1 Peter 2:18-25; 4:12-19

SUFFERING

LEARNING MENU

Remember that persons have different learning styles: visual, oral, sensory, and so forth. Activities that accompany each Dimension in the study book offer several ways of helping learners to experience growth through Bible study. Choose a variety of activities that will meet these learning styles. Be sure to select at least one activity from each of the three Dimensions.

Session Goal

Christians, like all other people, know that suffering is a part of life. There undoubtedly will always be discussion of the relationship of suffering to the Christian faith. Some still believe and teach that suffering is deserved, the consequence of sin. Others see suffering as a part of God's plan for our growth.

The goal of this lesson is to better understand the importance of our response to our own suffering. While suffering is not God's intention for us, God has allowed the conditions that cause it to exist in the world. How then will we respond when we find ourselves in painful circumstances?

Members of the class will be able to relate to this topic through sharing their experiences of individual suffering. Some will have been part of communities that have suffered.

Dimension 1:
What Does the Bible Say?

(A) Answer and discuss Dimension 1 questions.

1. It is not God's will that any should suffer, but we do. First Peter 2:19-20 makes it clear that we do not have God's approval simply because we suffer. But when we suffer unjustly, when we "do right and suffer for it," we are assured that God is with us. There is no reward for endurance if suffering is the consequence of wrongdoing.

This passage is directed to slaves, whose lot as possessions of their often cruel masters was deplorable. Peter lets them know that suffering at the hands of a harsh master does earn them God's approval if it is unjust suffering.

The same principle applies to us, regardless of the reason for the suffering. If we suffer as a result of doing good, God's gives us divine approval. If suffering is the result of our wrong deeds, we should not expect God's vindication.

2. One of the great promises of Scripture is revealed in 1 Peter 2:23-25. We are healed because of Christ's wounds on the cross. Although often we think of healing as the cure of our physical bodies, this act of Christ heals our sins, and therefore, our souls. The context of the verse is the suffering that comes from sin. Since Jesus bore our

sins in his body on the cross, his sacrifice makes us whole again after being separated from God by that sin.

3. Rejoice! That is the reaction 1 Peter 4:13 calls for when Christians suffer. Because of the promises of God as revealed in Christ, and the rewards that come when we suffer unjustly, we should "be glad and shout for joy." While we do not glorify suffering, we see the glory of Christ revealed in that suffering, and we rejoice in the assurance of God's promise of vindication and restoration, if not in this life, then in the next.

4. The "spirit of glory" in 1 Peter 4:14 is God's Holy Spirit. Some ancient manuscripts of this letter call this the "spirit of glory and of power." Since the persons of the Trinity, historically known as Father, Son, and Holy Spirit, are expressions of God, this means that we who suffer for Christ's sake have God with us.

(B) Discover the source of hope.

- Read over 1 Peter 1 and look for all the images, words, and phrases that sound "otherworldly" (such as verse 4).
- Distribute Bible dictionaries and commentaries.
- Form small groups of two or three and ask each group to look up the images they don't understand.
- Mention that the source of our hope, seen especially in difficult times, is that our eternal God, through the eternal Christ, has a secure and loving place prepared for us. Though suffering may be the rule in certain earthly circumstances, God will not allow the faithful to languish in such pain indefinitely. The lamb without blemish or defect (19), who is Jesus Christ, through his act of self-giving, is the source of our hope and faith.

Dimension 2: What Does the Bible Mean?

(C) What makes a martyr?

- Ask the class to review 1 Peter 4:12-19 as well as "A Modern Martyr" and "New Testament Persecution" on pages 77-78 in the study book. The information in "Dangerous Life and Times" on pages 109-112 of the study book will be useful as well.
- Consider the situation of the early Christian martyrs and those who suffered for the faith.
- Then create a list of people the class would consider martyrs in this century. A strict definition of martyrs is that they are persons who were put to death for their faith. The class might redefine martyr to include those who have been persecuted, tortured, or injured for the faith, but have not been killed. Some martyrs may be well-known in the world; others might be local persons, known only to a few.
- Divide into four groups and provide four sheets of poster

paper with markers for each group.

- Ask each group to write the answer to their question on the paper or the chalkboard. The questions follow:
—Group 1: What characteristics do these ancient and modern martyrs possess?
—Group 2: What risks do martyrs take in order to be faithful to their cause?
—Group 3: What are the attitudes of martyrs toward life and death?
—Group 4: What have these ancient and modern martyrs contributed to the ongoing faith in our behalf?
- Allow enough time for the groups to complete the task. Gather together and ask the groups to comment on the words and ideas listed. If the names of additional martyrs are suggested as the discussion continues, list these also.
- Conclude with a time of prayer, thanking God for the witness of the martyrs and courage for those who presently suffer for the faith.

(D) Remember your own baptism.

The act of baptism was important to the early Christian community. This sacrament bound them together in the faith. First Peter 3:21 presents baptism as an important act that God provides in response to the suffering in the world, tied to the suffering and resurrection of Jesus.

The Protestant tradition has often been casual about baptizing persons into the Christian family. In the last two decades, there has been renewed commitment to the deep meaning of baptism as the point of entry into the family of Christ, that is, the church.

Class members have two options, this activity and activity (E), to consider the significance of their own baptisms and the baptisms of others in the church.
- Reread "A Holy People" on page 78 in the study book.
- Ask each person to meet with one other member of the class. Encourage each pair to share stories of their own baptism. Many people will have to rely on the family stories they have heard since they were too young to remember themselves.
- If group members cannot tell about their own experience, invite them to talk about a baptism that was special to them, such as the baptism of their children, a friend, or a baptism in another tradition, done differently from theirs.
- Draw the larger group together. Ask them to discuss what they have learned from sharing stories.
- Discuss these questions:
—What are some of the traditions around your baptism or those of other traditions?
—Is there something missing when some members cannot recall their baptism?
—Compare the differences between private baptisms, done at home or after church, with those celebrated

with the congregation at worship. What are the differences and similarities?

—How could the church help the occasion of one's baptism to be more memorable?

(E) Study the baptismal liturgies.

● Form small groups and have available copies of the liturgy for baptism used in your tradition (*The United Methodist Hymnal*, "Baptismal Covenant II," pages 39-44). Most liturgies ask questions of those being baptized or of the parents and sponsors who present an infant or child for baptism.

● Turn to the questions in "Renunciation of Sin and Profession of Faith" on pages 40-41 in the *Hymnal*. Ask each small group to consider the questions. What do they mean?

● When the group is sure of the meaning of the questions being asked, discuss what it means to be faithful to those vows.

● Use these questions to sustain the discussion:

—How does a Christian live faithfully, seeking to fulfill the vows of baptism?

—What does it means to take these same vows on behalf of another, a child, or godchild?

—How can parents nurture their children in such a way that the children choose to be confirmed and accept for themselves the faith?

—What is the role of a sponsor or godparent?

TEACHING TIP

This would be good opportunity to plan a service of baptismal renewal, if such is available in your tradition. This might be celebrated in the class or in a service for the whole worshiping community.

Members of the class might be willing to care for each other by remembering each other's baptismal day. In the same way that we often remember birthdays, send a special note on the occasion of another person's baptismal anniversary. Recognize in class those whose baptismal anniversaries are to be celebrated in that week.

It would also be appropriate to plan a special party or social occasion to celebrate the joy of baptism or of baptismal renewal.

(F) Investigate rules for family order.

● Reread "An Obedient People" on pages 78-79 in the study book and 1 Peter 2:18–3:7.

● Do a "then and now" comparison with the advice given to households of 1 Peter's day and how households are ordered today. Have a Bible commentary and dictionary available to study more in depth these ancient roles.

● When you have identified the rules for family order, compare them. Ask:

—Who might be the equivalent of household slaves today (if anyone)?

—In light of the Bible passage to accept all authority, including harshness, would excessive control over a member of the household be acceptable today? Why? Why not?

—How are these roles different from the ways in which our society generally orders the household? How are they similar?

—How compelling is the biblical instruction today?

—If your household rules and relationships are different from what the Bible suggests, are they wrong? Give a reason for your answer.

(G) Who is the suffering servant?

First Peter 4 concentrates heavily on the role of suffering; 1 Peter 2:18-25 concentrates on Christ as one who suffered purposefully for us.

● Review "A Committed Community" on page 80 in the study book.

● Provide commentaries and ask the group to look up Isaiah 52:13–53:12, the last of four servant songs. (The others are Isaiah 42:1-9; 49:1-6; and 50:4-11.) These servant songs are interpreted in the New Testament community as passages that prophesy the suffering of the Messiah.

● Discuss these questions:

—How is the suffering servant in Isaiah like the Christ that 1 Peter portrays?

—What does that mean to you? What difference does it make in your life that Christians believe that Jesus Christ suffered on the cross?

—How is that suffering purposeful? What makes any suffering have positive meaning?

—Many persons suffer to the point of casting off their faith. How do you interpret that rejection of faith?

Dimension 3: What Does the Bible Mean to Us?

(H) Examine the meaning of suffering.

Two fine books that examine suffering and God's will are *When Bad Things Happen to Good People*, by Harold S. Kushner (Avon, 1983) and *The Will of God*, by Leslie D. Weatherhead (Abingdon, 1976). These works deal with the questions most persons struggle with in their own experience and in the way that they perceive the world.

- Check with class members to see who has read either of the books. Ask one person to present a book review, summarizing the pertinent points made by the author.
- Ask another person who has read one of the books to prepare two or three questions to get the discussion started.
- Divide into smaller groups for discussion. Have them read "Why Does God Permit Suffering" and "What Suffering Produces" on page 81 in the study book.
- Ask each group to try to come to a mutual understanding of what the Christian faith has to offer to the issue of suffering and its meaning for our lives.
- Invite the groups to consider the differences between what appears to be unmerited suffering and the suffering that is clearly imposed through sinful behavior. They should look into the Scripture references in those two study book sections for help.
- Ask:
—How do the rich cause the poor to suffer?
—How do ethnic or racial groups cause those not in their group to suffer merely because they are different?
—Where and how does the church have an impact on the causes of needless suffering?
—Is there such a thing for persons other than Christ to have "needful" suffering? Give a reason for your answer.

TEACHING TIP
This same activity could be used in an extended session or in a social setting in someone's home, especially if group members wish to read or reread the books and do a longer-term study.

(I) Reflect on new issues for our time.

Many Christian groups are presently considering the ethical dilemma created by the use of medical technology that prolongs physical life (and potentially, the physical suffering) of persons with terminal illnesses, prolonged pain, or endless coma. The suffering for such persons and their loved ones is more than physical, for there is often in these situations great mental anguish and spiritual struggle.
- Examine your church's stance on the use of medical technology, such as "Death With Dignity" (*The United Methodist Book of Discipline–1992*, ¶71.J, page 93). Read also "Faith in the Midst of Suffering" on pages 81-82 in the study book.
- Invite a resource person from the church to be present to help the class interpret the issues. Use this information as a basis for class discussion.
- Expand on the activity by studying the same issues in other contexts. Invite a speaker on living wills and current medical technology. Compare the consideration of

the issue in the church with the trends in the secular society.
- Ask:
—Do you agree or disagree with the denominational stance? Give a reason for your answer.
—What does the church have to contribute to the deliberation of sensitive issues surrounding suffering and death?
—What faith issues are involved?
—Have you and your family discussed your own wishes? If not, how might you start a conversation?

(J) Understand your "cross to bear."

Many of us have heard others talk about some daily or regular duty as their "cross to bear." They may be referring to caring for a difficult relative, having children in and out of trouble, recurring personal problems, or a host of other trying circumstances. There is a difference between coping with difficult circumstances, suffering, and suffering for the sake of Christ as 1 Peter describes.

Jesus told his followers that true discipleship includes taking up one's cross daily (Luke 9:23). By this he meant that we should be willing to suffer and die, if necessary, for the sake of the gospel, which is what Jesus did. First Peter captures this same intent on the true meaning of suffering. Daily aggravations are not crosses to bear, they are daily aggravations.
- Draw out three columns across the top of a large sheet of paper and put these three categories as abbreviated titles: "Difficulties," "Suffering," and "Suffering for Christ." Let them stand initially at face value; don't explain them yet.
- Distribute markers and ask each person to fill in examples of each category.
- Then open a discussion by asking participants to describe what they think is the difference among those categories.
- Continue the discussion by looking more closely at the examples to see how well they fit the category and why they were chosen as examples. Mention the information in the two introductory paragraphs as a means to further the conversation.

(K) Know suffering firsthand.

The best way to understand suffering in a Christian context is to know personally a Christian who suffers.
- Encourage class members to visit, perhaps in groups of twos or threes, persons they know who suffer physically or emotionally, yet are able to express their Christian faith.

- When you visit these persons, explain that you are studying biblical passages about suffering. Ask them to tell their stories, especially the parts related to their suffering. It might be good to write down some short quotes from the person being visited that summarize that person's faith.
- Focus on the persons being interviewed; then thank them for their time and wish them the best. Leading a closing prayer would be appropriate.
- Most persons who make such visits come back buoyed by the experience. Share in the larger group the experiences you have had and compare the responses you received from the persons who suffer with the verses about suffering in 1 Peter.
- If appropriate, devise an action plan so that class members can both continue to learn from persons who suffer and minister to their needs.

Closing Prayer
O God, we acknowledge that our world is a place where there is suffering. Sometimes we are the ones who suffer; sometimes it is those we know. Others whose names we do not know suffer this day. We pray for them, even as we pray for those near us and for ourselves. Forgive us when we are the cause of needless suffering for others. Forgive those who cause us to suffer. Help us to open our lives ever more to your grace in good days and in bad, the times of joy, and the times of sorrow. Amen.

Additional Bible Helps

Suffering
Not just in 1 Peter, but throughout the New Testament, suffering is an important theme. It is summarized in the *Encyclopedia of Biblical Theology*, edited by Johannes B. Bauer (Crossroad, 1981) as follows:

"The words of Jesus concerning the necessity of suffering are also echoed throughout the entire New Testament in the life of the faithful. Probably the Jewish idea is also present, namely that suffering is a means of divine chastisement or discipline (Heb 12:4-11; Rev 3:19), that it is a test by which the believer must prove himself (Rom 5:3f; I Pet 1:7), and for this reason the christians should rejoice over their sufferings (Jas 1:2-4; I Pet 1:6). But this is not the specifically christian understanding of suffering, the theology of which has been developed above all by Paul. The many sufferings which the christians encounter they endure 'for the sake of the name of Jesus' (Acts 5:41), and in imitation of his example (Heb 12:1f; I Pet 2:20f)."

For the Sake of Christ
Jesus said: "If any want to become my followers, let them deny themselves and take up their cross daily and follow me. For those who want to save their life will lose it, and those who lose their life for my sake will save it. What does it profit them if they gain the whole world, but lose or forfeit themselves?" (Luke 9:23-25). He was attempting to explain the dailiness of sacrifice required of a faithful disciple. All life has its daily hassles, but to be a follower, one must "pick up his cross daily." This is no frivolous comment or task.

For Jesus to pick up his cross, he had to be committed to die on it. Indeed, during his time of prayer in the garden of Gethsemane, Jesus knew he had to choose; would he be willing to take up a cross or was there a way to avoid the consequences of radical faith? We know the answer to that, not only in the Crucifixion, but in the Resurrection.

But while Jesus' suffering to atone for the sins of humankind ushered in a new era of salvation, it did not put an end to suffering. The Epistles are a significant testimony to the difficult days the early Christians faced. In an era of persecution, when just admitting to be Christian could mean a death warrant, suffering was part of the dailiness of life. These Christians suffered for the sake of Christ so that the gospel would not die, even if they did. Like Jesus Christ, they were willing to give everything, and not only suffer *for* him, but *like* him.

This much is probably evident from the letters studied throughout this volume of JOURNEY THROUGH THE BIBLE. What may be less evident is that these martyrs and persecuted Christians also suffered *with* Jesus Christ, who continues to suffer for the sake of humankind. We are called to participate in this dynamic relationship with Christ as well.

As long as any suffer, all suffer. As long as there is any injustice in the world, all are in captivity. As long as any are deprived of love, all are diminished. While we in complacence may forget, God still suffers for the sake of any who are not completely whole. As participants "in the divine nature through him," we have called to our memory the least and lost. Then we become partners not only in the suffering of Christ, but we are thus empowered to be the agents of change. This is what ennobles suffering for Christ, like Christ, and with Christ.

11

2 Peter 1:3-8; 3:8-10

GOD'S PROMISES

LEARNING MENU

Remember that persons have different learning styles: visual, oral, sensory, and so forth. Activities that accompany each Dimension in the study book offer several ways of helping learners to experience growth through Bible study. Choose a variety of activities that will meet these learning styles. Be sure to select at least one activity from each of the three Dimensions.

Session Goal

A key goal in this lesson is to consider the traditions that have shaped our faith and values. All persons are products of heritage, history, personal experience, culture, and community.

All this needed to be sifted by members of the first century church. Contemporary Christians likewise need to understand what has brought them to the present moment in their growth as Christian disciples.

Knowing from where we come is a step toward knowing where God is leading us. For us, the threat of persecution and the intensity of speculation on the nature of Christ coming again may not be the same as for the congregation addressed in 2 Peter. However, it is still important to clarify the essence of faith and purpose. What is our mission? our vision for the future? Is our vision in harmony with God's purpose?

TEACHING TIP

Responses may be very different among the individuals in the class. Each person is to be valued, understanding that the past has shaped us all. Each person is equally called by God into the future. One must not judge the correctness or value of the heritage of anyone in the class.

Dimension 1:
What Does the Bible Say?

(A) Answer the Dimension 1 questions.

1. Second Peter 1:3 makes it clear that God will give us *everything* needed for life and godliness. The reasons for God's gift are mentioned in subsequent verses. Rather than tell the congregation that they should just believe in God and everything will ultimately be all right, the writer mentions the reasons or consequences for recipients of this "divine power": goodness, knowledge, and self-control are not just attributes or indicators of a godly life; they are the tools to achieve it. By accepting God's divine power to change our lives we avoid being "ineffective and unfruitful" so "entry into the eternal kingdom of our Lord and Savior Jesus Christ will be richly provided for you" (1:11).

Make certain that class members realize the promise is about everything that is needed, not everything that is wanted. As we come to know Jesus, we have all that we truly need for a godly life.

2. The way to live a good life is listed in 2 Peter 1:5-7, but the reward precedes this list of qualities. In 2 Peter 1:4, the reward is to "escape from the corruption that is in the world because of lust" and to "become participants of the divine nature." It is no less than becoming like God. Instead of being caught in the whirlwind of satisfying our body's desires, we can become like Jesus, who empowers us to be divine.

3. There is no difference with the Lord between one day and a thousand years, according to 2 Peter 3:8. All time belongs to the Lord, but God reckons time differently from humans. *Kairos*, a term for eternal, godly time is distinct from *chronos*, the measurable minute-by-minute time we use to identify the passage of days. For God the distinctions we make between present time and eternity have no meaning.

4. God and the writer realize that persons who are anxious about their lives will have an immediate need to "see things happen," hopefully for the better. Although distinctions of time do not matter to the Lord, we are assured that God has compassion on our situations and that we do not need to wait forever for the Lord to fulfill divine promises. Second Peter 3:9 makes it clear that the Lord will not be slow about such promises. The verse implies that the Lord will wait for us to repent in order for us to receive the benefits of such promises.

5. Second Peter 3:9 states with certainty that the Lord does not want anyone to perish, waiting for all to come to repentance. Although the day of the Lord will come like a thief, at an unknown time (2 Peter 3:10), our patient Lord wants all to receive the divine promise that comes through repentance.

(B) Wait for the end.

Because 2 Peter has a vital feeling component about God's promises and the second coming of the Lord, try to engage class members in getting into touch with their feelings about Christ's second coming. Since this second coming is often referred to as the "end of the world," because of new heavens and a new earth that will be created (2 Peter 3:13), it can evoke fear and apprehension in us.

The emphasis in 2 Peter on God's promises is a positive reaction to an emotional subject—the impending coming of the Lord. For the author, the Lord's coming was to fulfill the promises that God had made in Jesus Christ, and therefore was something to celebrate, not something to fear.

TEACHING TIP

Sharing in Bible study classes can be done at two levels: the head level and the heart level. The head level is the thinking, rational way, reflecting with the mind on what is being discussed.

The heart level is the feeling mode, tied to our emotions more than to our thinking. It is much harder for most members of groups to share feelings than to share thoughts.

Some participants may openly discuss their own feelings or the feelings of others about our coming passage of time into a new millennium and the possible end of the world, either from environmental disaster or a religious happening such as the second coming of the Lord.

Do not get lost in a discussion of the details of the second coming of Christ. Be sensitive to how class members react to this subject and, as leader, ask questions that use the word *feel* to stimulate the discussion.

- Bring to class an assortment of recent newspapers or news magazines. Try to have enough so that no more than two people are looking at the same publication.
- Ask group members to search for headlines or news clippings that might indicate how we are living in "end times." Focus on articles or headlines that analyze the state of our current world and how the future looks.
- In addition to the headlines, you might also ask for examples of how television, movies, and music currently reflect images of what life will be like in the twenty-first century or beyond.
- List these images. (Make a montage of clippings if you have time and supplies to do so.)
- Now ask class members to skim through 2 Peter for passages that refer to the second coming of the Lord.
- Invite comments from group members on their discoveries. As they report to the rest of the class, ask them to minimize details and to reflect primarily on how they *feel* about the topic.
- Discuss these questions:
—What images have you identified?
—What emotional states do you suggest or predict?
—How do you feel about the possibility that the world may end?
—Do you think the end is imminent? Give reasons for your answers.
—What feeling do you have when you think of God's promises being completely fulfilled for you, as 2 Peter discusses?

Dimension 2: What Does the Bible Mean?

(C) False teachers beware!

- Review the information in the box "Gnosticism and Stoicism" (page 86) and "Be Prepared!" on pages 87-88 in the study book.
- Form three teams and assign one of these passages to each team: 2 Peter 2:1-3; 10b-16; and 17-22.
- Ask the teams to identify all the trigger words and phrases that characterize all false teachers and the writer's attitude about them. List these words and phrases on poster paper.
- Display the list and then ask these questions:
—What impression do you get of the false teachers?
—What is their influence (or potential influence) on the community of faith?
—What reasons do the faithful have to fear these false teachers?
—What does the writer see as their deserved "reward"? (See also 2:4-10a.)
—What should faithful Christians expect if they are swayed by this teaching?
—What should they expect if they hold fast to the faith?
—If you were even momentarily in doubt about some core faith belief, do you think these characterizations would fit you? that the consequences would be appropriate for you? Give a reason for your answer.

(D) Talk about our traditions.

Some of the situation in 2 Peter was a result of the diverse religious and philosophical backgrounds of the early Christians. They had come from Greek and Roman religions and from the Jewish tradition. While they held in common the life-changing experience of Jesus Christ, they would often seek to blend the old traditions, beliefs, and practices with the new.

In addition to the natural tendency to syncretism (blending culturally specific practices and beliefs), the practice of Christianity itself had moved from its roots in the tradition of the Jewish faith to a countercultural movement.

This situation is true for us as well. We come to faith from a variety of traditions and experiences. It is important to know who we are as we grow in faith. It is equally important to know what we hope to preserve and what must be discarded as God calls us into the future.

- Divide into groups of three. Ask each person to talk with the other two about traditions that are a part of their experience. These may include family, cultural, and religious traditions, some of which are tied to holidays and

others to significant family events such as baptisms, weddings, and funerals.
- It will be helpful to identify the nature of each tradition. For instance, there are some family traditions that relate to faith but may be as much cultural as they are religious.
- After identifying the traditions that are formative for the participants, ask them to look at the traditions in terms of those that help with growth in the Christian faith and those that may stunt or block such growth in Christian maturity.
- Bring the small group conversations back to the larger group and discuss together these questions. You may want to summarize ideas on the chalkboard.
—Which traditions need to be reshaped in today's world?
—What traditions in the life of the church help in faith development?
—Which, if any, hinder faith development?
—Are there traditions that have been lost that should be reclaimed? Which ones? Why should they be reclaimed?
—Are there others that should be discarded? Why?
—Which traditions in the secular world are in conflict with the Christian faith? How do they conflict?

(E) Analyze a valedictory.

The author of 2 Peter wrote a testimonial or valedictory to the congregation. He may have believed that, for him, death would or could come soon. This may be his last opportunity to reach the church.

- Ask group members to look at "The Last Testament" on page 88 in their study books.
- Have them read 2 Peter 1:3-21.
- Provide pens and self-adhesive note pads. Distribute at least fifteen or twenty notes to each person.

TEACHING TIP

If you have a large class, form smaller groups to do the same exercise. Each group can post its notes on different walls of the classroom.

Or, divide the Scripture passage so that small groups are working on different portions of the testimony. Each person may not need as many self-adhesive notes.

- Give the group five minutes to write in their own words the essential points of Peter's testimony, *one point to a note*. These points do not have to be in any particular order as long as there is only one brief item, such as "God gives us promises" or "God's gifts keep us effective" on each self-adhesive note. Do this in silence.
- Still working in silence, randomly post all the notes on a wall, chalkboard, or window where everyone can read and reach them. Give class members three or four minutes in silence to rearrange the notes so that similar ideas

are together. Anyone can move a note, and notes can be moved more than once.

● When the notes are clustered, break the silence by asking them to decide on a title or category that labels each cluster of similar items, such as "Reasons for Hope" or "Gifts of God."

● Then analyze the total picture that emerges to identify what Peter found most important to include in his testimony.

Dimension 3:
What Does the Bible Mean to Us?

(F) Get ready to prepare your own valedictory.

● Review together "A Final Message" and "Your Last Message" on page 89 in the study book.

● Ask the members of the class to imagine that they are being asked to address the congregation for the last time. Suggest that they use the testimony in 2 Peter 1 as a model.

● If you did not do activity (E), review 2 Peter 1:3-21 and ask this question:

—What are the main points that this writer felt were important to cover? Think about what they mean to you.

TEACHING TIP
Activities (G), (H), and (I) are three steps of the process identified in "Your Last Message" and briefly introduced in activity (F). Consider doing all three of these activities in sequence.

(G) Identify who is God and what God has in store.

● Look at "Who God Is" and "A Look at Your Future" on page 90 of the study book.

● Distribute a copy of *The United Methodist Hymnal* to each person. Ask them individually to search for hymns and prayers that give them insight into the identity of God. As a place to begin, suggest looking in the "Index of Topics and Categories" under the headings of "Adoration and Praise," "Jesus Christ," "Kingdom of God," "Holy Spirit," or "Presence (Holy Spirit)."

● Ask participants to write down or to note for their own use the images, names, and characterizations that convey to them who God is and what God is like. Have them add any other images from the Bible that are meaningful to them.

(H) Examine things you know for sure.

● Focus on "The Promises You Know" on pages 90-91 of the study book.

● Review your findings from activity (E) or (F).

● Spend a few minutes to do this activity now, but encourage class members to continue this for a one-week period. Ask participants to keep with them a notebook or journal.

● Ask these questions:
—What are God's promises?
—What are God's promises to you?
—How does God keep the promises that God has made?
—What evidence do you see in your own life that God is keeping promises made to you?

● Encourage each person to jot down any thoughts, experiences, or questions that relate to these questions.

● Remind the class that we are persons of faith in every context, not just at church. As disciples, we are to learn to pray without ceasing (1 Thessalonians 5:17). It is equally important to learn to reflect upon faith at all times and places.

● Ask any person who wishes to do so to share their journaling at the following week's session.

(I) Write your own valedictory.

● Look over "A Plan of Action" on page 91 of the study book.

● Let each person write a testimonial or message to the church. Allow fifteen minutes for this project.

● Suggest that class members keep in mind all the images, insights, and learnings that have surfaced throughout the session. In addition, invite them to keep in mind these questions:

—What is the impact of turning to issues of faith in the world of every day?

—What new insights do you have to share on the ways in which our faithful God makes and keeps promises with God's sons and daughters?

● If participants are willing, have them read their testimonials to the class. If class members give permission, you might include some testimonials in the church newsletter, along with an explanation of the project.

(J) God is calling.

● As the class concludes, play quiet music. Ask everyone to sit comfortably and to close their eyes in order to allow a brief time for silent, prayerful reflection.

● Now ask each person to be aware of the pattern of his or her breathing. Remind them that breath is life and is a gift from God. Invite them to breath deeply in a relaxed way and to breath out slowly. Allow some time for this attitude of relaxed breathing to settle in.

● Read or paraphrase the following guided meditation. Pause where indicated so participants can reflect on the images that come to mind.

Let go of any worries or stress that you have brought with you to class . . . This way of relaxing in silence is a way to prepare to listen to God. God seeks to come into our lives and to speak with us . . . .

Imagine being in a place that is peaceful for you . . . . It can be anywhere that you feel close to God, indoors or outside . . . . Now picture Jesus coming toward you. Observe what he looks like . . . . Anticipate his presence . . . .

Now you can see Jesus clearly. As Jesus comes closer to you, you can see that he is smiling; he is very happy to see you . . . .

Jesus comes very close and sits near you . . . . He tells you that you are very precious and very much loved by God . . . . Notice how you feel about that message . . . . What is the expression on his face? . . . What is Jesus doing as he tells you this wonderful thing? . . .

Jesus now begins to speak to you about your gifts for ministry . . . . He reminds you that your gifts are given by God. What gifts does he mention? . . .

Jesus then speaks to you about using your gifts for ministry. He reminds you that you are chosen and called into service . . . . He shares with you a way in which your special gift is needed in creating a future where God's love and justice will be the way of life for all . . . . Notice how you feel about that . . . .

Jesus rises to go. As he does, he takes your hands and gives you his blessing. . . .

- As the directed meditation ends, invite participants to take a few more seconds to breath slowly while they take the time they need to return to the classroom setting.
- Ask participants to divide into pairs and to relate, if they wish, any insights they might have received during the meditation. No one has to discuss his or her experience.
- As class members are willing, discuss the following questions. These questions may also be used in the journaling exercise during the coming week.

—How do you perceive that God is calling you to use your gifts?

—What might be God's call of ministry and service for you into the future?

TEACHING TIP

The use of guided meditation is very effective for some, but not for all. This should not discourage you from trying it from time to time. This activity encourages the functions of both mind and spirit, as participants develop the inner life of spiritual formation.

The two questions provided in the text after the meditation could be used to introduce this activity, either as discussion starters or as points for private reflection. Consider using them before the guided imagery if you want to use the meditation as a devotional exercise.

Closing Prayer

Loving God, we give you thanks and praise for the gift of your Son Jesus Christ. We pray that as we know him more clearly, we will see more clearly how our lives imitate his. Focus us on our mission and bring clarity to our vision for the future. And in all that we do, keep us in harmony with your vision for your church. We ask in the name of Christ. Amen.

Additional Bible Helps

What is a promise in the biblical sense? *The New Bible Dictionary*, edited by J. D. Douglas (Inter-Varsity Fellowship, 1962; page 1036), describes it in part in the following way:

"A promise is a word that goes forth into unfilled time . . . . A promise may be an assurance of continuing or future action on behalf of someone. . . . It may be a solemn agreement of lasting, mutual (if unequal) relationship: as in the covenants. It may be the announcement of a future event: 'When you have brought the people from Egypt, you will serve God on this mountain'. The study of biblical promises must therefore take in far more than the actual occurrences of the word. . . .

"That what He has spoken with His mouth He can and will perform with His hand is the biblical sign manual of God, for His word does not return void. Unlike men and heathen gods, He knows and commands the future. . . . Through the historical books, a pattern of divine promise and historical fulfillment is traced, . . . expressive of this truth.

"The point of convergence of the Old Testament promises (to Abraham, Moses, David, and the Fathers through the prophets) is Jesus Christ. All the promises of God are confirmed in Him. . . . Jesus is its guarantee. . . and the Holy Spirit of promise its first installment. . . .

"Awaiting the promise of Christ's coming again and of new heavens and a new earth. . . , the Church sets forth on her missionary task with the assurance of His presence. . . and with the news that 'the promise of the Father'—the Holy Spirit. . . —is given to Jew and pagan in Jesus Christ, fulfilling the promise to Abraham of universal blessing through his posterity."

GOD'S LOVE IN US

1 John 3:18-23; 4:7-21

LEARNING MENU

Remember that persons have different learning styles: visual, oral, sensory, and so forth. Activities that accompany each Dimension in the study book offer several ways of helping learners to experience growth through Bible study. Choose a variety of activities that will meet these learning styles. Be sure to select at least one activity from each of the three Dimensions.

Session Goals

The goals of this session are to more fully understand the fullness of Christ in both divine and human dimensions and to explore in some depth the diversity of meaning that we call love.

Dimension 1:
What Does the Bible Say?

(A) Answer and discuss Dimension 1 questions.

1. "We receive from him whatever we ask" is the proclamation of 1 John 3:22. How can this be so? The key is in the last part of the same verse. When we obey God's commandments and do what pleases God, what we ask is the same as God's will. The ancient Christian saying from Augustine, "to love God and do as you please," is another way of stating the truth in this verse. When we truly love God, our desires are changed by God so that what we want is what God wants, and therefore God is able to give us all that we ask.

2. The command to love one another comes from God, according to 1 John 3:23-24. God's commandment is to believe in the name of Jesus and to show that belief by loving one another. The strength to do this comes from God abiding in us.

3. Those who are born of God and know God are the ones who love one another, according to 1 John 4:7. First John 4:8 states this in a different way: those who do not love do not know God, for God is love. We can tell the ones who know God by the way they show God in their day-to-day activities.

4. First John 4:12 says clearly, "If we love one another, God lives in us, and his love is perfected in us." The unconditional, overflowing love of God that we know because God lives in us is made perfect in us. Therefore, God's perfect love is in the world, in us and through us. Perfect love is also mentioned in 1 John 4:17-18.

5. The same perfect, divine love that we know (see question 4) is what casts out fear, according to 1 John 4:18. If we fear, we have not reached perfection in love.

When fear of judgment is gone, it is evidence of God's perfect love in us.

(B) Decide between human or divine love.

If your class members leave with any understanding that God's love comes through them or with any appreciation for the possibility that perfect love can be expressed in their lives, you have learned well what 1 John expresses. Christians believe that God is love and that love demonstrated is an expression of God's love. Even persons who do not believe in God or who do not want to be identified with God in any way can still be used by God as an instrument of love. To deny this is to limit God.

- List on a board or newsprint these qualities in two columns: human and divine.
- Have class members tell stories that show love. Encourage them to use personal stories rather than anecdotes they have only heard from someone else.
- After each story is told, pause to reflect with the class members, then ask these questions:
—Is the love that was shown in the story human love or divine love?
—How would you define human love? divine love?
—What passage from 1 John supports your definitions?
- After several stories have been told, and you have listed these qualities for all to see, reflect on the meaning of human and divine love. If you had difficulty distinguishing whether a particular act of love was human or divine, you understand 1 John. First John presents love as coming from God, but expressed in us.

Dimension 2: What Does the Bible Mean?

(C) Look for God's love in a diverse world.

- Review "How to Love in a Diverse World" and "Enthusiasm and Diversity" on pages 93-94 in the study book.
- Then ask class members to skim through 1 John to look for instances of contrasts between good and evil or for other dichotomies. (See also the Additional Teaching Helps in this chapter.)
- Ask these questions:
—What examples of diversity can you find in 1 John?
—Are there any instances where this diversity is considered good? Give examples to support your answer.
—What examples of diversity do you see in your church?
—In your opinion, are these examples of diversity good for the church? for the faith? for individuals? Give reasons for your answers.

—In keeping with the words from the Scripture and from the teachings of the church, what place does diversity have in the church? Do you agree? Why?
—What is the meaning of unity in diversity?
—How can we be one when we are so different?

(D) Test the spirits.

- Read over "False Teachers" on page 95 in the study book, with special attention to the box on docetism.
- Read also 1 John 4:1-6, which gives a basic rule for discerning between what is of God and what is not.
- Have students identify the rule and talk about what it means until you are satisfied they understand it. Pull out some pieces of information from the study book reading and ask participants to indicate which things are of God and which are not.
- Then ask:
—How do you discern what is of God and what is not from the list of situations and characterizations that follow? The important issue is to learn *how* one discerns, rather than arriving at a specific answer. Ask class members to add other items.
—"an eye for an eye";
—the death penalty;
—a parent who significantly limits a child's activity to protect the child from harm;
—using God's name to defend abortion;
—using God's name to defend right-to-life;
—private or home schooling to avoid integration;
—giving money to a homeless person who is probably alcoholic;
—transplanting an organ to an elderly person.

(E) Respond to the fullness of Christ.

- Divide the class into three groups. Ask each group to do a research project on the life and ministry of Jesus, the Christ.
- Provide Bible dictionaries and concordances, especially topical concordances.

Group 1. Body
- This group is to use the Synoptic Gospels (Matthew, Mark, and Luke) to review some of the events and teachings that emphasize the physical well-being of Jesus, both for himself and in his ministry with others.
- **Where to look:** Instruct this group to check passages that mention Jesus eating and needing rest (such as his participation in Passover meals, the Temptation, his meals shared with tax collectors, grain plucked on the sabbath, going to a quiet place to pray, sleeping in the boat, and so on). Passages that refer to healings provide ample evidence of Jesus' ministry to the physical well-being of others. There are also passages in which Jesus

teaches us about the human needs that we have and the truth that God cares about those needs.
- **What to do:** Ask someone to record the passages cited and a few brief words about the content of each.

Group 2. Mind
- This group is to look for passages in which Jesus taught and encouraged people to use their minds. Jesus challenged the authorities to grow in their capacity to understand more of God as they stretched their minds.
- **Where to look:** One wonderful image of Christ using his mind is the passage in Luke 2 when Jesus became separated from his parents and was found at the feet of the rabbis. The parables are another starting point. Some Bible dictionaries under the heading "Parables" will list all the references. Look also for passages where Jesus engaged and challenged the scribes, Pharisees, or Sadducees in conversation.
- **What to do:** Have someone record the passages cited and a few words about the content of each.

Group 3. Spirit
- The group is to look through John 1 and 1 John for emphases on the divine nature of Christ that was always there. This is the meaning of the existence of Christ before his taking human form.
- **Where to look:** There are other passages that indicate the Spirit of God in Christ. Point the group to accounts of the Transfiguration (Luke 9:28-36) and Jesus' ascension following his resurrection (Acts 1:6-11).
- **What to do:** Ask group members to look for any indication of the spiritual nature of Christ. Have someone record the passages and a few words about the content of each.

- As the groups complete their research, draw them back to the whole group.
- Using a large sheet of paper or a chalkboard, write these three headings at the top of each of three columns: "Body," "Mind," and "Spirit."
- Ask each group to report. List the passages and a few words about the content of each.
- As the activity is completed, remind the class that Christianity affirms that Jesus Christ is fully human and fully divine. While the fullness of this truth may remain clouded in mystery, we who seek the presence of Christ in our lives relate to his fullness as we respond to him in our humanity—body, mind, and spirit.

(F) Review the idea of God's love for all.

- Provide several copies of the "Social Principles."

- Review "Is God's Love for All?" on page 97 in the study book.
- Look in 1 John for passages that indicate whether God's love is inclusive or exclusive. Discuss any passages that seem unclear.
- Then review the church's position on various issues as stated in the Social Principles. This review can be done individually or in small groups assigned to different sections.
- Discuss the statements as you ask these questions:
—How is love present in this statement?
—What forms has love taken in formulating this particular statement or stand on the part of the church?
—Are there other ways that love could be enhanced with regard to this issue?
—How would you change the statement to reflect your understanding of God's love?
—Are there ways in which this statement seeks to include all people in the circle of God's love?
—Is there a way in which someone or something seems to be excluded?
- If the group has divided into smaller units, draw back together to compare your findings.

Dimension 3: What Does the Bible Mean to Us?

(G) Is love all in a word?

This activity is designed to study the word *love* in order to understand the diversity of its meaning. Remind the class that the English language uses the word *love* in many ways.

- Have available dictionaries, Bible dictionaries, and a thesaurus or two.
- Brainstorm for two or three minutes and record as many "love" statements as you can. Each person should call out as many ways as possible of how we use the word *love*. Use the powerball approach if you wish. (Review the Teaching Tip on page 40 in session 8.) Record the responses.
- Then mention the three Greek words that relate to types of love (each with a different meaning).

> - *Eros*—commonly thought of with regard to bodily love, libido, sexual desire.
> - *Philia*—fondness, sentiment, liking, attachment. This type of love is often associated with friendship.
> - *Agape*—spiritual love, Christian love. This Greek word is used to describe the self-emptying love of God and the sacrificial love of Christ, especially as it is presented in Philippians 2. Agape love is a love that allows us to seek the well-being of the other person without regard to our own reward or even our own safety.

- Put these three Greek words and meanings on the board or poster paper.
- Decide which of the three words applies to each of the examples of love mentioned during the brainstorming.
- Then use the dictionaries to look up as many words associated with love as you can find. There are whole sections in a typical thesaurus on meanings and concepts related to the word *love*.
- Add the words and meanings to the list on the chalkboard or on the paper. Using the word study as a background, ask the class to discuss the following questions:
—In what ways is our common understanding of *love* too limited?
—How does a limited understanding of love affect our actions? our relationships with other people? our regard for and treatment of the poor? our expressions of justice?
—How should the Christian faith through the church offer a greater understanding of love to the community? nation? world?
—Are there ways in which our church needs to grow in demonstrating love within the congregation? in the community?

(H) Look for love.

- Look again at "What Love Is" on pages 97-98 in the study book.
- Have available newspapers and magazines, scissors, and tape.
- Ask class members to look for stories in the papers or magazines that illustrate the presence of love or the lack of it. Remind the class of the broad meanings of the word love.

- Ask each person to show the picture or article they have found and to tell the reasons that it depicts love or the lack of love. Post the articles and pictures in the room or on poster paper.
- Spend some time in discussion of the articles and pictures:
—Which, if any, of the items from the list in "What Love Is" pertain to the picture or article? Why do you think so?
—When and where is love most present in society?
—How is family life in our country affected by our understanding of love?
—Is our present time a good time in which to live with regard to love and justice? Give a reason for your answer.
—What could have been done or what could be done to bring God's love to the situation where love is lacking?
—How can we become more active in demonstrating love and justice in the name and spirit of Christ?

(I) Put love in action.

- Review "The Bounds of Love" on page 98 in the study book.
- Ask class members to mention again some of the ways in which they have been specially loved and nurtured. Now that you have been immersed in biblical concepts of love, ask them to indicate what biblical passages reflect the ways they have experienced this love.
- Discuss ways the individuals, the class, or the church could develop specific ways to show love in return.
- Ask the class to spend some time in prayer and reflection, making sure that some of this time is spent in silence. In this silence, class members will be able to listen to God, who speaks often in the silence of our hearts. God calls us as individuals to acts of love. God also calls the community, as in a group such as this adult class.
- Begin to share ideas of what the class might do as an act of love.

TEACHING TIP

The needs are great wherever one looks. There may be a project in the world mission of the church that is not currently a part of the church program. The class might want to invite persons engaged in special ministries to come and point out the needs in missions here or away from home.

The "Teaching Tip" in activity (F) suggests a church or class project. Individuals may wish to take on a special project of their own. A personal project may be passive, as in a commitment to prayer or study for particular persons or subjects or in practicing "random acts of kindness" when the occasion presents itself. The project could be active, as in a one-on-one ministry as a mentor or personal companion.

If you choose a group project, decide by consensus (the process of listening and discussion that allows everyone to be heard and taken seriously, even if all do

- When the class has completed the project, evaluate it using these criteria and others you identify:
—Did class members grow in the capacity to love through the activity? Is this something that should be continued? If so, how?
—What have we learned about the nature of God's love?
—How will members of the class continue to open themselves to the presence of God's love in their own lives, and God's call in Christ to love others as we love ourselves?

Closing Prayer

O God, you come to us as love. You assure us that we can never be separated from the love you offer to us in Christ. We thank you for that perfect gift. We acknowledge that from time to time we choose to separate ourselves from that love through our thoughts, our words, and our deeds. We seek your forgiveness and your healing. Restore us in those times of separation; help us to hear your call to new life. We seek to grow in grace. Through the love of Christ, we pray. Amen.

Additional Bible Helps

A Study in Opposites

First John is a study in opposites: the life of love versus the life contrary to love. John begins his thesis using the images of light and darkness. In that era, especially with the gnostic influences, light and darkness had similar connotations to good and evil, radical love and radical sin.

In chapter one and into chapter two, John carefully lays his foundation and reinforces his points throughout the Letter. This message is not new; it has been present "from the beginning" (1 John 1:1-2) and can be verified through our senses (2:7-8). Since the faithful have seen and heard, they are in a qualified position to testify to the truth of the gospel (1:3; 5:14-15). This is no idle testimony, but one that brings joy (1:4), fellowship (1:3), guidance for living and protection from sin (1:6-8; 2:1-2; 5:18-19), forgiveness (1:9), and eternal life (5:11-12, 20). There is no hiding place for persons who profess to live in this light, but who in reality live in darkness. God knows who lives in truth and who does not (1:10; 2:3-6, 9-11).

A New Commandment: Love One Another

God is love (4:7-16) and thus is the origin of love wherever love is shown. One proof of this love is in the person and sacrifice of Jesus Christ, who willingly gave up his life for our salvation (4:10). In grateful acknowledgment of such a gift, we are to love others. We are capable of learning from the biblical examples of love and of the direct love shown to us by others what true love is (3:11-16). In fact, if we see the needs of the world and do not help, we deny God's love (3:17).

This love of God and the sacrificial gift of Jesus Christ make us God's children (2:28–3:3) who once and for all time live in God's love as God's love lives in us (3:18-24).

Do Not Love the World

In contrast to the great love of God, born of the Spirit and demonstrated in personal and practical ways, we are to put off the sinful nature that occurs in the world—pride, greed, lust, and whatever else separates us from a right relationship with God (2:15-17). We are warned of the consequences of falling into the trap of worldly sins and the snare of false teachers (2:18-27; 3:4-10).

To protect ourselves, John suggests a rule of thumb to help us discern what is true and what is false (4:1-6). Every spirit that confesses Jesus Christ and whose actions support the assertion are from God. All else is falsity and error.

The Ultimate Conquest

Lest we be overwhelmed with the enormity of discerning the spirits and fighting against the forces of evil, we are assured that we have a faith sufficient to conquer the world (5:1-5) and a perfect love that casts out all fear. Does this mean that a Christian living in fearful times should never be afraid?

While John empowers us with the armor of faith in the battle with evil, he does not presume that "local" fear disappears. With God's help, evil will be overcome, even if the momentary occasion is frightening. But for the faith community, what may be more frightening is coming to the Day of Judgment and finding that our love has been insufficient. As God's children who obey the commandment to love, the fear of eternal judgment is swallowed in perfect love (4:17-21).

John offers one last admonition to underscore this point: "Little children, keep yourselves from idols" (5:21). If we keep just this one command, we live forever in God's great love.

13

2 John 3-11;
3 John 11;
Jude 17-23

WARNINGS

Remember that persons have different learning styles: visual, oral, sensory, and so forth. Activities that accompany each Dimension in the study book offer several ways of helping learners to experience growth through Bible study. Choose a variety of activities that will meet these learning styles. Be sure to select at least one activity from each of the three Dimensions.

Session Goals

The goals of this lesson are to understand some of the concern expressed by the writers of 2 and 3 John and Jude in holding fast to the faith in the congregations of the early church, to experience issues of the church and faith today that may be similar to those in the late first and early second centuries, and to explore some of the specifics of the Letters in this chapter in light of the joys and struggles of early Christians.

Dimension 1:
What Does the Bible Say?

(A) Answer and discuss the Dimension 1 questions.

1. Deceivers, according to 2 John 7, are those "who do not confess that Jesus Christ has come in the flesh." Therefore, the opposite is also true. Persons who truly have God in their lives are the ones who proclaim that God has come to earth as a human being known as Jesus. Second John 9 goes further, stating that it is those who continue in the teaching of Christ who have both the Father and the Son in their lives.

2. Third John 11, like the Book of James, says that those who are from God are the ones who do good. Those who do evil are the ones who have not seen God. Belief is not enough; good deeds are needed as proof that those who claim God are truly from God.

3. Worldly, divisive people are those devoid of the Spirit, according to Jude 19. They are the ones who are "indulging their own ungodly lusts," according to Jude 18. Without God's spirit, the author contends, they create divisions, especially in the church.

4. Mercy, not judgment, is called for by the author of Jude 22, for those who are wavering in the faith. This mercy is modeled by none other than Jesus Christ, who shows mercy to us (Jude 21).

(B) Heed warnings.

- Assemble before the class as many symbols or physical signs that imply a warning as you can find, such as
—a red traffic light;
—a "Mr. Yuk" poison sticker or skull and crossbones;
—traffic signs such as "Do not enter" or "Detour";
—a red line drawn through a symbol, such as a non-smoking sign with a red line drawn through a cigarette.
- Form three groups and have class members look for warnings in 2 John, 3 John, and Jude.
- List these warnings on large sheets of paper or chalkboard and discuss the possible situations in the early church that led to these concerns.
- Consider whether your church needs to heed the same warnings as the first century church.
- Ask:
—What warning signs would you post in your church building?
—What concerns do you have for the church of today?
- Then ask the class to think of other warnings and lead into a discussion of various things that are dangerous, such as
—a teenager suddenly dropping old friends and beginning to associate with less reputable persons;
—someone who suddenly has lots of cash, although there is no change in employment or income;
—a spouse who withdraws, refusing to talk;
—an active church member who stops coming to worship and other activities with no explanation.
- Ask these questions:
—What message in the Bible equips us to deal with these social warning signs?
—What message from the Bible helps us offer words of hope; concern; comfort; or, when necessary, confrontation in these potentially dangerous situations?

Dimension 2:
What Does the Bible Mean?

(C) Sort through conflicts.

- Review "Warning! Warning! Warning!" on pages 101-102 in the study book.
- Ask the class to identify the conflicts that plagued the early church (differing cultures, philosophies, religious roots; the mystery religions; discouragement; waning zeal).

- Ask for three or four volunteers to "stand on their soapbox" to make a plea for members of the faith to recognize these sources of conflict or potential conflict. (One person might even take on Cerinthus!) The plea should balance the need to stand firm with the danger of simply rejecting whatever is different as "wrong." Some conflict is healthy, especially when it leads to conversation and understanding.
- After each person steps down from the soapbox, discuss briefly these questions:
—What were the main points of the plea?
—How did they support the faith?
—How well did they respect alternate views while maintaining the Christian faith?
—What new insight did you gain from the speech?

(D) Watch out for deceivers.

- Review the section "2 John" and at least the first two paragraphs of "3 John" on page 103 in the study book.
- Assign 2 John 7-11; 3 John 9-12; and Jude 5-13.
- Discuss these questions:
—What are the characteristics of these deceivers?
—How might they be recognized?
—Why should we not "let them in the house"?
—Is there, do you think, any hope that deceivers might become true believers? Give a reason for your answer.
—Who might we identify as deceivers today? (Be careful about naming specific people.)
—What would we do to keep these current deceivers out of the house?
—What would that mean if we take seriously a ministry of reconciliation?

(E) Identify authority figures.

- Review "3 John" on pages 103-104 in the study book and the comment on Diotrephes in 3 John 9-10.
- Though most are not mentioned by name, identify in the greetings of 2 John and Jude those who are considered authoritative within that faith community.
- Ask for a few volunteers to prepare and act out a brief skit or drama that illustrates some or all of the following points or that answer the questions:

Point 1
There were persons in each of those house churches who competed for the loyalty of individuals and congregations. There were those who claimed to be the accepted authority as leaders of each of the groups.
—Who was to be trusted with authority for the fledgling church?
—Who held the truth in teaching and in practice?

Point 2
Members are warned about false teachers and leaders, and urged to remain loyal to the true faith.
—What is the true faith?
—How are they to know truth from falsehood?

Point 3
We humans seek to invest some with authority and leadership. This we know we need so that there will be order and not chaos.
—Who then do we look to as authoritative for us?
—To whom do we listen?
—Which persons or groups command both our attention and our allegiance?

Point 4
We don't always have confidence in leaders whom we select.
—Should members of the clergy be looked upon as authoritative simply because they hold the positions of pastor and priest?

TEACHING ALTERNATIVES
Suggest that class members do some research during the week. Invite group participants to choose a person or group that many people would consider authoritative. Ask them to find out all that can be discovered about that person or group during the week. They may be from the religious or secular community.

If the authority figure is on radio or television, be sure that someone can listen or watch and report back.

Group members may need to consult other resources to find out about their choice of authority. They may use newspapers, libraries, books, and experts who know the persons or groups being researched.

As class members prepare to report back the next week, offer the following questions as guidelines for reflecting on the persons they discover:

—Who are these persons or groups?
—When and how did they come to a position of power and influence?
—Who are their followers?
—What do they teach?
—What do they expect from those who follow their leadership?
—Does the authority and intended influence of this person or group reflect the life, teaching, and Spirit of Jesus Christ? If so, in what ways? If not, why not?

(F) Discover Enoch.
• Have on hand several Bibles that include the Apocrypha and a copy of the Pseudepigrypha, if you can

find one. Your pastor might have it, but you will probably need to check with a good public library or a theological library.
• Read "Jude" on pages 104-106 in the study book and look up the references to Enoch in the Bible and in the other books, if possible.
• From the information about Enoch that you can find, answer these questions:
—What is Enoch's message to the faith community?
—How might you define *scoffers*, *grumblers*, *malcontents*, *flatterers*, *libertines*, and *worldly people devoid of the Spirit*?
—What is the "fire" from which wavering Christians need to be snatched?

Dimension 3: What Does the Bible Mean to Us?

(G) Make a clear witness.
• Review "Today's Warnings" on pages 106-107 in the study book. Keep in mind the affirmative nature of most of the content of 2 John, 3 John, and Jude.
• Ask class members to pretend that they are ambassadors from the church to areas that are foreign to them. (Since the true church generally stands in contradiction to much of society, this should not be too hard to imagine.)
• Ask ambassadors individually or in teams of two or three to choose a "mission field" to visit with the message of Christ and the (universal) church of Christ. A "mission field" might be the entertainment industry; big business; institutions of higher learning; or groups of people, such as homeless persons, incarcerated persons or their families, substance abusers, and so on.
• The ambassadors should determine the nature of their witness in their chosen mission field. Ask them to jot down notes about how they will approach their task.
• Ambassadors should consider these questions as they prepare:
—What seem to be the needs in this mission field?
—How can I speak my message without being "turned off"?
—What is the most winning way to approach this mission field?
—How can I show respect without necessarily agreeing with what is contrary to my message?
—How could the church strengthen its witness within this segment of the community?
• If you have time, ask for volunteers to take on the role of persons in the mission field and interact with the ambassadors.
• Discuss the plans of action.

(H) Write a letter of warning to your church.

- Review "The Prophetic Role" on pages 107-108 in the study book.
- The prophets will write their own letter of warning to their church. Have available paper and pens in order to facilitate the activity.
- Set the scene by designating each person as a prophet concerned about the life of the church, now and in the future. Since they cannot be present with the congregation, they intend to send a letter. The congregation has expressed a need to hear from their leaders and has promised to carefully consider what the letter will say and suggest.
- Some class members may know exactly what they want to write. Others might look at ideas or categories to be considered in the content of the letter. Suggested topics include
—The levels of apathy and commitment in the present ministry of the congregation.
—The meaning of sin and evil in the church and world.
—Conflict within the congregation and the ways that conflict is handled.
—Issues of morality and ethics in Christian life and in the church.
—Family relationships and Christian values.
—Teachings and beliefs. Is the congregation holding fast to the faith as taught by Christ?
—The outreach of the congregation in witness and service. Is the church centered on service to self or to others?
- Give the prophets time to write. Obviously, they will not be able to cover every point on the above list.
- Ask volunteers to read their letters and discuss their main points as time allows.

(I) Be a winsome witness to your church.

A pastor once used the term *winsome* as he talked to people in his parish about witnessing. The author of Jude seems to doubt the depth of faith on the part of those who may read the letter.

We are well aware that there are many levels of faith as well as apathy and doubt concerning commitment to the Christian faith. To those whose lives have been changed and are continuing to be changed through the love of Christ comes the holy calling to invite others to share the joy of God's grace in Christ. How do we do this in our contemporary world?

To be winsome in one's witness is to invite others to experience God's grace, love, and justice. Few are those who respond to threats and fear.

- Post the words *winsome* and *invite* on the board or on a poster.
- Ask the class to consider what a witness that is both win-

some and invitational might be like as offered to others in these areas of the ministry of the church. Focus on your local congregation as you ask these questions:

—How can worship be offered in such a way that all persons, including seekers and newcomers, feel included?
—Is the program of the church in education, mission, and outreach a program that witnesses to the love of Christ and invites others to become a part of it?
—Is there a place for everyone of both genders and of all ages, cultures, languages, and abilities in the circle of fellowship of the congregation?
—How are newcomers offered a place in the fellowship?
—Does the congregation need to start new groups to invite seekers to become a part of the fellowship of the church?
—Does the church extend its witness to those often excluded from the church?
—What needs to happen in the church in ministry with the poor? with youth who seem to be drifting in today's world?
—How can the church be winsome in its witness to those outside the community of the church?
—What must the church be and do in order to strengthen its ecumenical witness to the community in your area?
—How can the church strengthen its witness within national life?
—How can the Christian faith tradition strengthen its collective witness to the world community?

(J) Celebrate your love in Christ.

A strong theme in this study has been the need to be strong in the faith and centered in the life, death, and resurrection of Jesus Christ. This faith is the life of the church. Christians who hold fast to faith and who witness to the power of God's grace in Christ are bound together in the love that is in Christ and is Christ.

It would be good to conclude the study with a celebration of that love. *The United Methodist Book of Worship— 1992* has several suitable liturgies: "Reaffirmation of Faith" (page 86), "Covenant Renewal Service" (page 288), Services of Daily Praise and Prayer (pages 568-580), or "The Love Feast" (page 581). The class might choose to share in a love feast, if this has not already been done.

A social occasion of fellowship and fun would be appropriate. Perhaps the class would like to invite others to participate. Consider including newcomers, seniors, youth, children, another class, a group outside the church.

The essence of the love feast is to share a meal, as simple as bread and water, while singing songs of faith and having various persons share the story of their faith.

The spirit of the event is to celebrate the joy of God's people. What we celebrate is our response to God's desire to love us into becoming the incarnation of that love, which is the fullness of God in Jesus, the Christ.

Closing Prayer

God of the centuries, you come to us and reveal yourself through the church that you love. Through our baptism, we have become a part of the church. Through us, you share your grace with a world that hurts and hungers in body and in spirit. Your son, Jesus Christ, tells us that we are to offer gifts of love and justice in his name. Sometimes we hesitate because of what we may risk. Sometimes we hesitate because following Christ may cost too much. Sometimes we are weary. Sometimes we want it to go our way and not yours. Please help us to open our lives in trust that you will fill us with wisdom, energy, and courage. Please stay with us as we grow in grace and in commitment to your vision for your people and for your church. In the name and spirit of your Son, the Christ. Amen.

Additional Bible Helps

The contributions of the three letters highlighted in this chapter are noted in the following two writings:

The Letters of 2 and 3 John

From *Harper's Bible Commentary*, edited by James L. Mays (HarperCollins, 1988; pages 1290-91):
"2 John and 3 John were probably written at about the same time as 1 John, but they are letters to sister churches. 2 John is addressed to 'the elect lady and her children,' while 3 John is addressed to Gaius, a member of a congregation that had received travelers sent by the elder. From these letters we gain further information regarding steps the elder was taking to prevent the dissension from spreading to other congregations in the constellation of Johannine churches.

"The Johannine Letters continue to have value for both historical and theological reasons. Because they cast light on a chapter in the history of the Johannine community, the Letters allow us to read the Gospel of John with greater insight. They expose both the strengths and weaknesses of Johannine theology and record the problems to which that theology was vulnerable. As a collection and individually, the Letters also provide a tragic reflection on the hostility and distortions that are created by schisms and divisions within the church. Their greatest value, therefore, may be realized as a by-product of their original purpose: they may help the church to recognize the destructive effects of divisions within the Christian community."

The Letter of Jude

The contribution of Jude to New Testament thought, according to Merrill C. Tenney, is expressed in the following excerpt from *New Testament Survey* (William B. Eerdmans Company, 1985; pages 373-74):
"The epistle shows that by the time it was written, quite certainly no later than A.D. 85, there was a recognized body of belief that could be called Christianity. Doctrinal formulation is a slow process, and the history of Christianity for the last nineteen hundred years is the history of the rise and fall of doctrinal patterns and emphases, some of which were extreme, others of which were erroneous, but all of which belonged to the general stream of thought that is called Christian. One would be tempted to think that these variations might be inconsequential were it not for the fact that the New Testament sets certain rigorous doctrinal standards. Some leeway may be allowed for human ignorance and for intellectual and spiritual limitations . . . . In these epistles, however, which were written when error was prevalent and controversy was beginning, there is a frank insistence on 'the pattern of sound words,' and Jude speaks with finality of 'the once-for-all-delivered-to-the-saints faith' (Jude 3, literal translation), which was to be kept as an inviolate standard.

"The proper method of treating those who deviate from this standard is also given in Jude. Nowhere does the New Testament recommend persecution or burning at the stake for heretics. The heretics draw their own lines. . . . The epistle, instead, counsels mercy and an attempt to rescue those who are deluded and bewildered, though no tolerance is to be shown to the falsehood itself."

Colossians—Jude at a Glance

The chart below may help you sort out quickly when and by whom a book was written (if known) and the major theme. Two dates are provided for each book; the first is generally accepted in conservative theological research; the second in liberal scholarship. All the New Testament books are listed so that the books of this volume can be noted in their context of the whole canon. Some of the dates presume that certain books were actually pseudonymous and are marked with a question mark. Authorship is noted only for the books covered in this volume.

BOOK	DATE		AUTHORSHIP	THEME
1 Thessalonians	**47-53**	**50-51**	Paul	Pastoral letter of concern; assurance about the end times
2 Thessalonians	**47-53**	**50-52 or 65-70**	Paul	Same as 1 Thessalonians
Romans	54-57	54-57		
1 Corinthians	54-55	54-55		
2 Corinthians	55-57	55-57		
Galatians	55-60	53-56		
Ephesians	54-64	80-100?		
Hebrews	**54-68**	**75-95**	Unknown	Hold fast to the covenant with God; follow Christ's example; learn from the heroes of the faith
James	**55-62**	**100-125**	Brother of Jesus?	Encouragement; care for the poor; doing works of faith; living an upright life
Colossians	**56-60**	**56-60**	Paul	**Divinity AND humanity of Christ**
1 Timothy	**58-67**	**95-105?**	Paul (?)	Teaching on faith, law, sound teaching, church order, and good works
2 Timothy	**58-67**	**95-105?**	Paul (?)	Same as 1 Timothy
Titus	**58-67**	**95-105?**	Paul (?)	Encouragement; warnings about false teachers
Philemon	**58-67**	**95-105?**	Paul (?)	Pastoral concern about Onesimus
Matthew	60	80-90		
Mark	60-70	70-80		
Luke	60	85-90		
Philippians	60-64	54-58		
1 Peter	**63-64**	**90-100**	Unknown (Disciple Peter?)	Faith in the midst of suffering
2 Peter	**64-68**	**125-150**	Unknown (Disciple Peter?)	Defense of Christianity against its critics; warnings about false teachers
Acts	80	85-90		
Jude	**80-100**	**100-125**	Brother of Jesus?	Appeal for faithfulness; guard against false teachers
1 John	**85-95**	**90-110**	Disciple John	Mandate to love God and one another; test the spirits; show hospitality to fellow Christians
2 John	**85-95**	**90-110**	Disciple John (?)	Same as 1 John
3 John	**85-95**	**90-110**	Disciple John (?)	Same as 1 John
Revelation	85-95	90-95		
John	90	90-100		

⁍HE SOCIAL WORLD

BY ABRAHAM J. MALHERBE

Travel and Communication

One of the first things to strike one about the Roman world is its mobility. Probably not many people traveled as much as the Phrygian merchant whose epitaph claims that he had visited Rome seventy-two times, but travel was not at all unusual, especially for merchants and artisans who followed their business and trade.[1] Travel by sea had become relatively safe and regular, but since sailing virtually ceased between mid-November and mid-March, the highways carried most of the traffic. The Roman system of highways, originally constructed to serve the needs of the military, brought people to Rome in such numbers that Roman critics became alarmed.[2] The Christian tentmakers Aquila and Priscilla, variously located in Pontius, Rome, Corinth (Acts 18:1-3), Ephesus (Acts 18:18, 26; 1 Cor. 16:19), and Rome again (Rom. 16:3), fit this picture well, as do the more than two dozen people Paul greets in Romans 16, whom he had evidently known in the eastern Mediterranean, but who at the time of writing had found their way to Rome.

As other religions spread along the highways, so did Judaism and Christianity.[3] For the most part, in the first century, particularly outside Palestine, Christianity took root in major cities, frequently provincial capitals, on the main routes. Its rapid spread was facilitated by a number of factors. People could communicate in the common *(koine)* Greek (see Acts 21:37), which had developed with the spread of Greek culture three centuries earlier during Alexander the Great's conquests. Latin was the official language, but local languages and dialects continued to be spoken (see John 19:20; Acts 14:11). The well constructed and drained highways, marked by milestones showing the distance to Rome, made it possible to cover about fifteen miles per day by foot, about twice as far by cart. Maps and guidebooks informed travelers of the sights and accommodations along the way. The latter consisted of inns located at convenient places on the highways, around public squares, and near important buildings in the cities. The conditions in the inns were not of high quality,[4] so, wherever possible, Jews, Christians, and well-off pagans availed themselves of private hospitality (see Acts 21:4-16).

These features associated with mobility affected people's lives and practices. Christians, for example, wrote in

Greek, and it is of special importance that letters became a favorite means by which people separated from each other kept in touch as well as gave and received instruction.[5] It is no accident that most of the NT writings are letters or have epistolary features and that letters are found in other writings (e.g., Acts 15:23-29; 23:26-30; Revelation 2–3).

Despite the abuse to which it was subject, hospitality remained a virtue among some pagans.[6] Among Christians it became a concrete expression of love for the church (Rom. 12:9-13; Heb. 13:1-2; 1 Pet. 4:7-11; 3 John 6–8). The Christian practice of providing food and lodging to travelers and of "sending" or "speeding" them on their way—i.e., to pay their traveling expenses—invited abuse. Some became freeloaders,[7] while others took advantage of Christian hospitality to spread heresy (see 2 John; cf. 1 John 4:1-3). In order to assist travelers in securing aid while exercising some control, a special type of letter, in which the writer recommended the bearer to friends or associates, had been developed.[8] Some Christians also wrote such letters (e.g., Acts 18:27; Rom. 16:1-2), and some churches evidently demanded them of travelers (2 Cor. 3:1).

Life in the City

Despite a tendency among the well to do to romanticize country life, the vitality of society was in the cities, and that is where Christianity flourished.[9] To the cities were drawn purveyors of goods, proclaimers of new divinities holding out promises of salvation, and moral reformers of every stripe. Merchants and artisans tended to settle in their own neighborhoods, so that customers knew where to shop for what (e.g., 1 Cor. 10:25, "in the meat market").

As diverse as the propagandists were, so were their methods of recruitment. Devotees of the Egyptian goddess Isis paraded in procession through the streets of Corinth on the way to the sea, but their initiations and other rites were performed in secret.[10] A huckster like Alexander of Abonoteichos founded his own cult by attracting public attention through his colorful behavior and playing on the credulity of the masses.[11]

Philosophers taught in their own schools and the salons of the rich or wherever they were invited to speak, and some of the more unscrupulous posted themselves on streetcorners or shouted in the marketplace, finding their way to wherever people gathered.[12] The picture that we have, often from writers who decried it, is of an openness to new teaching,[13] a phenomenon well known to Luke (see Acts 17:18-20).

There is very little evidence that Christians in the first century proclaimed their message in so public a manner. The major exceptions are Paul's preaching in Lystra (Acts 14:8-18) and Athens, but even in the latter instance, after the initial contact in the marketplace, Paul was taken to the relative seclusion of the Areopagus, where he delivered his sermon (Acts 17:17-21). Christianity may at times have been in the public mind, but it was not in the public eye.[14] The book of Acts describes Paul as first preaching in the synagogues and then moving his base of operation to private homes (e.g., Acts 18:4-8; cf, 17:1-6), and we frequently read of churches meeting in individuals' homes (e.g., Rom. 16:5, 23; Philemon 2).[15]

Most people in the cities lived in crowded quarters, some in houses on narrow streets, but more in apartments, which concentrated the population and severely limited privacy. In the hot Mediterranean climate, much of life was spent outdoors, making use of such facilities as public baths and sometimes toilets, buying meat from the market (1 Cor. 10:25), hot water from the tavern on the corner, having a dispute settled by a block organization, or shopping in the stores along the main roads or surrounding the central open square where official business was also transacted. Workers labored in small shops or workrooms, which might be part of houses (Acts 18:2-3; 1 Thess. 2:9); organized themselves into guilds; and entertained themselves by going out to dinner in a temple restaurant (cf. 1 Cor. 8:10) or in private homes (cf. 1 Cor. 10:27) or by attending plays, the races, or political speeches. Pressure could easily build up in the crowded neighborhoods, sometimes in response to mere rumor, especially when self-interest was at stake, and might result in stoning (cf. Acts 14:5, 19), something that children learned at play.[16] Then confused mobs would pour out of the alleys and streets into the stadium or forum where demagogues would work on them (cf. Acts 17:5-9; 19:23-41).

Social Groups

An important feature of city life during the early empire was the existence of large numbers of organized groups, formed to serve a variety of purposes.[17] Some of them were professional clubs (*collegia*) or guilds whose aim was not so much to improve the economic status of the craftsmen or tradesmen who organized them as to provide opportunities for social life. On occasion they engaged in political activities, and one of their major responsibilities was to bury their members. Few were completely secular; some were named after particular gods, whose names were carried on their clubhouses—for example, the "hall [*schola*] of the goddess Minerva." Sometimes these facilities were named after a club's patron; it is possible that

the hall of Tyrannus, to which Paul moved his activities in Corinth, was such a clubhouse.[18] In organization they resembled their political and social contexts, so that their members enjoyed a sense of order and a certainty of how they might advance in the organization. In addition to these clubs, other organizations, such as schools of various sorts, served similar if not entirely the same purposes; and religious groups, including at times Jewish synagogues, were accommodated politically, and must in any case have looked to outsiders like *collegia*.[19]

Like the Christians, these groups often met in the homes of patrons (see Rom. 16:2, 23), who thereby incurred legal responsibility for them (see Acts 17:5-9).[20] This type of extended household appears to have formed the social context for churches in the first century, and with important consequences. Some social and ethnic diversity was to be found in the pagan associations, but diversity was more common and pronounced in the churches, which therefore had to give serious attention to relations between their members. Such issues as the social stratification of the church and its accompanying social attitudes (e.g., 1 Cor. 11:17-34); the responsibilities of members of a family (e.g., Col. 3:18–4:1) and a church (e.g., Titus 2:1-10); and how Christians' social practices and religious observances should or should not influence their relations with each other (e.g., Rom. 14:1–15:7) required constant attention.

The more groups looked inward and focused on their peculiar identities, the more they were viewed with suspicion by the larger society. This was so, for instance, in the cases of the Epicureans and the Jews, who were each accused of atheism because they refused to worship the traditional gods and of misanthropy because they were thought to disdain people who did not belong to their own groups.[21]

Christians met with similar responses. Knowing that they could not escape the society in which they lived (1 Cor. 5:9-10; 1 Thess. 4:11-12), they were sensitive to how they were to respond to "outsiders" with whom they mixed socially (1 Cor. 10:27-29 *a*), who thought their worship sometimes crazy (1 Cor. 14:23), who badmouthed them (1 Pet. 3:9; 4:3-4, 14), who accused them falsely of crimes (1 Pet. 2:12), or who challenged their beliefs (1 Pet. 3:13-16), which were thought strange or new (Acts 17:9-21).[22] In the century with which we are primarily concerned, then, the issues touching these groups were mainly social criticism and ostracism.

Political Status

Roman authorities tolerated such groups as long as they were not socially subversive or did not upset the political order. When that did happen, the authorities acted with force, as they had acted against the Bacchanalians two centuries earlier[23] and would act again against the devotees of Isis[24] and the Druids.[25] Of particular interest for our

70

purposes is the Roman governmental attitude toward the Jews, for initially Christians were thought of as Jews (see Acts 18:12-15).[26] The Roman attitude differed from place to place and time to time, but was more positive than the local frictions, especially in Alexandria, and the popular slanders might lead one to expect. The Romans held in high regard the Jewish claim to venerable traditions and customs, and granted the Jews, at various times, such concessions as not requiring them to appear in court and allowing them to meet for worship on the Sabbath and to collect the Temple tax.

As Christianity became distinct from Judaism, it constantly had to fend off attacks, for it enjoyed no official recognition. These persecutions, however, were always local and in response to local circumstances until the Emperor Decius (249–51), in order to secure the goodwill of the gods, required everybody in the empire to sacrifice to the ancestral gods.[27] Decius's decree was not aimed specifically at Christians, but its practical effect was that Christianity was legally proscribed by imperial decree. Before Decius' decree, action was taken against Christians because they were charged with committing crimes (cf. 1 Pet. 4:15) or causing disorder (cf. Acts 17:6-7; 24:5), accusations that became associated with the name *Christian* even in the absence of proven guilt. But uncertainty about the status of Christians persisted for some time. So, for example, around 112 CE, Pliny, the Roman governor of Bithynia, even after attending a trial of a Christian, was still uncertain whether Christians should be punished simply for bearing the name or for the crimes that had evidently come to be associated with that name.[28] It need not surprise us that charges against Christians were made out of motivations ranging from economic (e.g., Acts 19:23-41) to religious competition (e.g., Acts 13:48-50; 17:4-8). As Tertullian observes, after demanding that Christian churches be allowed the same rights as *collegia*, it was easy to lay blame at their door: "If the Tiber rises as high as the city walls, if the Nile does not send its waters up over the fields, if the heavens give no more rain, if there is an earthquake, if there is famine or pestilence, straightway the cry is, 'Away with the Christians to the lions.' "[29]

More complicated was the veneration thought due the emperors and Christian reaction to it. The Roman attitude had its antecedent in Greek views. The Greeks did not distinguish sharply between the gods and extraordinary human beings, who, because of exceptional endowments and benefits they had rendered, achieved after death the status of heroes. They were considered semi-divine beings who were worshiped in the locations with which they had been associated in life. The stress on virtue as their divine quality suggested the possibility that by possessing virtue in this life, such a person, particularly a ruler, was worthy of veneration. When such veneration was associated with the ruler of a domain as extensive and

rich in diversity as the Roman Empire, complications were created for the ruler's subjects.[30]

Emperors in the first century differed on how they thought about their own divination and about what veneration they required or permitted. Tiberius (Luke 3:1; 20:20-26) resisted all veneration of himself, but Caligula (Gaius) proposed that Tiberius be deified and demanded that he himself, and later his sister Drusilla (Acts 24:26-27), be worshiped. His successor, Claudius (Acts 11:28; 18:2), refused such worship of himself, and rejected a request from the Alexandrians to appoint priests and establish temples in his honor. Nero, however, deified Claudius after his death and laid personal claim to many honorifics, such as acclamations of himself as god, savior, and lord. By the time of Vespasian and Titus, deification of the imperial family had become a common practice. Domitian, who exercised imperial power to the full in all aspects, insisted that he be treated as divine, and one's failure to do so resulted in punishment.

Throughout this period, more enthusiasm for the imperial cult was shown in the provinces than in Rome. There, prominent officials played major roles in the cult, so that it is difficult to be sure that participation in the cult was an expression of popular religious sentiment and not mere political expediency, as a way of currying favor with the emperor. Asia was a major center of the imperial cult after Augustus, and under Domitian venerated the emperor in a manner that called forth the description in Revelation 13.[31]

Education and Literary Culture

It is not possible to determine the level of literacy in antiquity with certainty, but perhaps half of the population of the Roman Empire could read.[32] since it was the custom to read out loud, however, even when by oneself (cf. Acts 8:27-30), the written word did not remain a mystery to people who could not read.[33] So the illiterate person could listen as someone read the Epicurean teaching inscribed on a long wall by Diogenes of Oenoanda or hear philosophers preaching on the street corners or declaiming in large public spaces to which they had been officially invited. The theaters further introduced the masses to drama, and professional orators were always ready to speak for a fee on a large stock of topics. The Greco-Roman world was highly oral, and that exercised a profound influence on education.[34]

Education progressed through three stages. In the first, pupils were given elementary instruction in reading and writing; in the second, they learned more about grammar and, in addition, language and literature; and in the third, which was more diverse, they could specialize according to their professional interests by placing themselves under the tutelage of the philosopher, a physician, or a lawyer. Professional philosophers and rhetoricians competed for the same audiences and scathingly denounced each other, but in the schools pupils received instruction in both rhetoric and philosophy, with rhetoric gradually coming to dominate the curriculum. Education made extensive use of handbooks, such as those summarizing philosophers' teachings[35] and collections from dramatists, especially Euripides and Menander, whose works were thought to be morally valuable.[36]

Very little explicit comment is made in the NT about the educational level of Christians. The description of the disciples of Jesus as unschooled and ordinary (Acts 4:13; cf. John 7:15) means that they had not received traditional and formal religious instruction. On the other hand, Paul's development is described in Acts 22:3 in the traditional three categories, and he is represented as quoting from precisely the kinds of sources that students learned in tertiary education.[37] In 1 Cor. 15:33 Paul himself quotes Menander, and in Titus 1:12 Epimenides, representing the same level of literary culture, is quoted. In the final analysis, however, the NT writings themselves constitute the main evidence of the literary culture of their authors. As one would expect, they differ considerably. Paul's letters reveal him as a creative writer knowledgeable of, but not bound by, the literary conventions, rhetorical methods, and philosophical instruction of his day. Matthew and Mark wrote in a Greek that must have struck their Gentile readers as strange, but the Greek of the book of Hebrews is excellent, as is that of those sections in Luke and Acts where the author does not reflect the style of his sources.

1. G. LaFaye, ed., *Inscriptiones Graecae ad res Romanas pertinentes* 4 vols. (Paris: Leroux, 1927) 4:290-91 (no. 841). See also W.M. Ramsay, "Roads and Travel in the New Testament," *HDB* 5:375-402: Lionel Casson, *Travel in the Ancient World* (Toronto: Hakkert, 1974).

2. E.g., Juvenal *Satires* 3.62: "The Syrian Orontes has long since poured into the Tiber."

3. See A.D. Nock, *Conversion* (Oxford: Oxford University Press, 1933) 48-98, for a description of how ancient cults spread.

4. See Horace *Satires* 1.5; *Acts of John* 60.

5. E. g., Seneca's *Moral Epistles*.

6. See Dio Chrysostom, *Oration* 7.

7. *Didache* 11.

8. See e.g., Cicero *Letters to His Friends*, Book 13.

9. For a dated but still useful description of one city, see Jerome Carocepino, *Daily Life in Ancient Rome* (New Haven: Yale University Press, 1940): for social attitudes of urban and rural folk, see Ramsay MacMullin, *Roman Social Relations, 50 B.C. to A.D. 284* (New Haven: Yale University Press, 1974); and for a description of urban churches, see Wayne A. Meeks, *The First Urban Christians; The Social World of the Apostle Paul* (New Haven: Yale University Press, 1983), and John E. Stambaugh and David L. Balch. *The New Testament in Its Social Environment* (Philadelphia: Westminster, 1986) 59-82.

10. Apuleius *Metamorphoses* Book 11.

11. Lucian *Alexander the False Prophet*.

12. See Dio Chrysostom *Oration* 32:7-11; cf. *Oration* 9.

13. E.g., Juvenal *Satires* 3:58-66, 109-25.

14. Nock, *Conversion*, 192. See also Stanley K. Stowers, "Social Status, Public Speaking and Private Teaching: The Circumstances of Paul's Preaching Activity," *NovT* 26 (1984) 59-82.

15. The fact that Paul's preaching in the synagogue is not simply a creation by Luke is indicated by 1 Cor. 9:20; 2 Cor. 11:24, 26; cf. Rom. 1:16.

16. See MacMullen, *Roman Social Relations*, 66.

17. See Meeks, *The First Urban Christians*, 75-84, for the different groups as analogies for the Christian congregations.

18. See Abraham J. Malherbe, *Social Aspects of Early Christianity*, 2nd rev. ed. (Philadelphia: Augsburg Fortress, 1983) 89-90. The NRSV rendering of the Greek *schole* into "lecture hall" is an interpretation that is almost certainly wrong.

19. Tertullian (*Apology* 38-39) would later demand that Christian groups be treated as legal associations. See Robert L. Wilken, "Collegia, Philosophical Schools, and Theology," in S. Benko and J.J. O'Rourke, eds., *The Catacombs and the Colosseum* (Valley Forge, Pa.: Judson, 1971) 279-86.

20. For the material and literary evidence of the physical space in which Jews, Mithraists, and Christians met, see L. Michael White, *The Social Origins of Christian Architecture*, 2 vols. (Minneapolis: Augsburg Fortress, 1993).

21. For attitudes toward the Jews, see Menachem Stern, *Greek and Latin Authors on Jews and Judaism,* 3 vols. (Jerusalem: Israel Academy of Sciences and Humanities, 1976-1984); for the Epicureans, see Plutarch *That Epicurus Actually Makes a Pleasant Life Impossible: Reply to Colotes* and *Is 'Live Unknown' a Wise Precept?*

22. See Robert L. Wilken, *The Christians as the Romans Saw Them* (New Haven: Yale University Press, 1984).

23. Livy 39.8-18.

24. Tacitus *Annais* 2.85.

25. Ibid., 14.30.

26. Cf. Tacitus *Histories* Fragment 5.

27. See G.E.M. de Ste. Croix, "Why Were the Early Christians Persecuted?" *Past and Present* 26 (1963) 6-38; and A.N. Sherwin-White, *Past and Present* 27 (1964) 23-33.

28. Pliny *Epistles* 10.96, 97.

29. Tertuillian *Apology* 40.1.

30. See Donald L. Jones, "Christianity and the Roman Imperial Cult," in W. Haase and H. Temporini, eds., *Aufstieg und Niedergang der romischen Welt* (Berlin: De Gruyter, 1980) 2.23.2, 1023-54.

31. Irenaeus (*Against Heresies* 5.30.3) dated John's banishment to Patmos, and thus the book of Revelation, to the reign of Domitian.

32. William V. Harris, *Ancient Literacy* (Cambridge, Mass.: Harvard University Press, 1989), the major study in the field, is very conservative in its estimate. Attempts to correct Harris are made by contributors to the collection. J.H. Humphrey, ed., *Literacy in the Roman World, Journal of Roman Archaeology* Supplement Series 3 (Ann Arbor: University of Michigan Press, 1991).

33. See Paul J. Achtemeier, "*Omne verbum sonat:* The New Testament and the Oral Environmental of Late Western Antiquity," *JBL* 109 (1990) 3:27.

34. See H.I. Marrou, *A History of Education in Antiquity* (New York: New American Library, 1964), for Greece and Rome, and for Concentration on the latter, Stanley F. Bonner, *Education in Ancient Rome: From the Elder Cato to the Younger Pliny* (Berkeley: University of California Press, 1977).

35. See pseudo-Plutarch *The Education of Children* 8C.

36. See Dio Chrysostom *Oration* 18:6-7.

37. See W.C. van Unnik, *Tarsus or Jerusalem: The City of Paul's Youth* (London: Epworth, 1962); and Martin Hengel, *The Pre-Christian Paul* (Philadelphia: Trinity Press International, 1991) 18-39 for Paul, and Malherbe, *Social Aspects*, 29-58, for a broader view.

From The New Interpreter's Bible, Volume 8, *Abingdon, 1995; pages 12-17. Used with permission.*

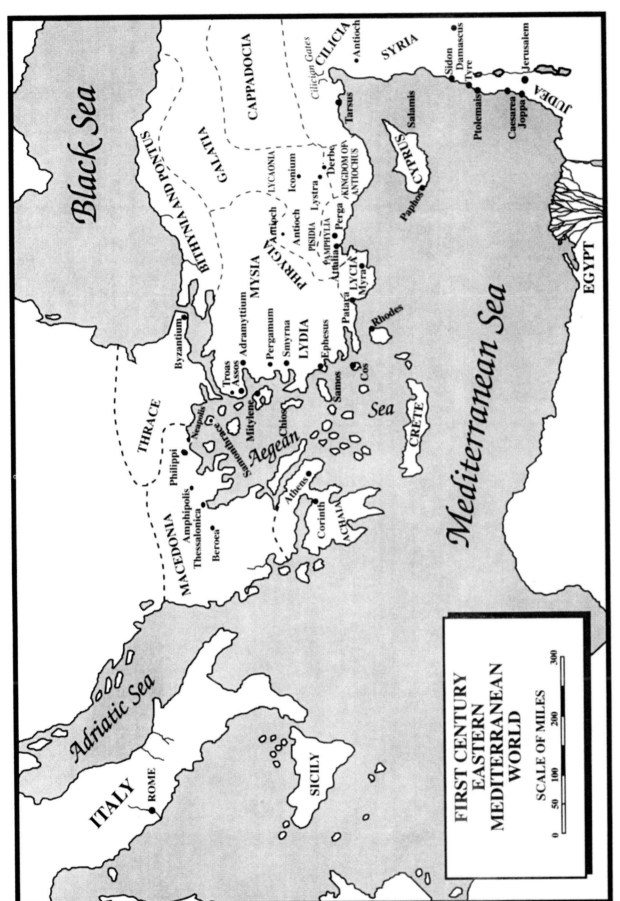

FIRST CENTURY
EASTERN
MEDITERRANEAN
WORLD

SCALE OF MILES

0   50   100   200   300

CPSIA information can be obtained at www.ICGtesting.com
Printed in the USA
BVOW051156260313

316497BV00002B/27/P